TAKE ME OUT

BY RICHARD GREENBERG

★

★

DRAMATISTS
PLAY SERVICE
INC.

For Lee Greenberg, Ed Greenberg,
Jon Greenberg, and Linda Pierce

ACKNOWLEDGMENTS

The author wishes to thank Irene Cabrera, Gene Gabriel, Robert M. Jiménez, and James Yaegashi for the translations.

TAKE ME OUT was originally produced by the Donmar Warehouse (Sam Mendes, Artistic Director) and the Joseph Papp Public Theater/New York Shakespeare Festival (George C. Wolfe, Producer; Mara Manus, Executive Director; Michael Hurst, Managing Director) in New York City, opening on September 5, 2002. It was directed by Joe Mantello; the assistant director was Trip Cullman; the set design was by Scott Pask; the lighting design was by Kevin Adams; the sound design was by Janet Kalas; the costume design was by Jess Goldstein; and the production stage manager was C.A. Clark. The cast was as follows:

DAVEY BATTLE .... Kevin Carroll
TODDY KOOVITZ .... Dominic Fumusa
RODRIGUEZ .... Gene Gabriel
KIPPY SUNDERSTROM .... Neal Huff
MARTINEZ .... Robert M. Jiménez
SKIPPER .... Joe Lisi
MASON MARZAC .... Denis O'Hare
JASON CHENIER .... Kohl Sudduth
DARREN LEMMING .... Daniel Sunjata
SHANE MUNGITT .... Frederick Weller
TAKESHI KAWABATA .... James Yaegashi

TAKE ME OUT subsequently opened at the Walter Kerr Theatre on Broadway on Feb 27, 2003. It was produced by Carole Shorenstein Hays and Frederick De Mann. It was directed by Joe Mantello; the assistant director was Trip Cullman; the set design was by Scott Pask; the lighting design was by Kevin Adams; the sound design was by Janet Kalas; the costume design was by Jess Goldstein; and the production stage manager was C.A. Clark. The cast was as follows:

DAVEY BATTLE	Kevin Carroll
TODDY KOOVITZ	David Eigenberg
RODRIGUEZ	Gene Gabriel
KIPPY SUNDERSTROM	Neal Huff
MARTINEZ	Robert M. Jiménez
SKIPPER / POLICEMAN / WILLIAM R. DANZIGER	Joe Lisi
MASON MARZAC	Denis O'Hare
JASON CHENIER	Kohl Sudduth
DARREN LEMMING	Daniel Sunjata
SHANE MUNGITT	Frederick Weller
TAKESHI KAWABATA	James Yaegashi

CHARACTERS

DAVEY BATTLE

TODDY KOOVITZ

RODRIGUEZ

KIPPY SUNDERSTROM

MARTINEZ

THE SKIPPER

MASON MARZAC

JASON CHENIER

DARREN LEMMING

SHANE MUNGITT

TAKESHI KAWABATA

TAKE ME OUT

ACT ONE

Kippy, solo.

KIPPY. The whole mess started with Darren, I suppose. After all, if he hadn't done the thing, then the next thing wouldn't have happened, or all the stuff after, and — but no, that's not right.
How could a "mess" have started with Darren?
Who would you ever less associate with that word?
After all: Darren Lemming. *(Darren appears in uniform.)* As if you don't already know:
A five tool player of such incredible grace he made you suspect there was a sixth tool. Something only he had. Something you couldn't name.
In addition to all the other stuff:
The one-man-emblem-of-racial-harmony stuff.
His white father. His black mother. Their triumphant yet cozy middle-class marriage.
Even in baseball — one of the few realms of American life in which people of color are routinely adulated by people of pallor, he was something special:
A black man who had obviously never suffered.
For a few years, he seemed to be the answer to every question.
So no: Mess does not flow forth from Darren Lemming. *(Fade out on Darren.)* In that case:
The whole mess started, I suppose, soon after the All Star break when our world-champion Empires, looking to glide into a three-peat, started losing close games in the ninth inning and we had to call up a closer from Double A Utica. And that closer, as you all now know, was ... Shane Mungitt. *(Shane Mungitt appears in uniform.)* A

man from whom mess *does* flow forth.

And so anyway, Shane came to us and …

But no … this is too abrupt. You need to know some stuff before I can get to Shane. You need a little *back*-story.

Okay.

The whole mess started in eighteen-something-something when Abner Doubleday (this never happened) gathered a group of friends into a sylvan vale and mapped out a diamond made of four bases set ninety feet apart and … No.

The whole mess started with a really beautiful *park*. And in the park were a man, a woman, a serpent, and this *tree*. And …

Okay. *(Kippy nods to Shane. Shane exits.)*

Convenience sake:

The whole mess started one morning when Darren Lemming said to himself: What the hell? I'm Darren Lemming and that's a *very good thing* … *(Lights on Darren flanked by team.)*

DARREN. Now I'm not a personal sort of guy, really, and that's not gonna be any different. I mean don't expect the free flow of information. Don't expect the daily update. I'm just here to play ball. I'm just here to have a good time. That's no different. But, you know, it seems like, you reach this certain level of achievement, everyone wants to know what's goin' on with you. The irrelevancies. And they're the fans so they have certain rights, certain limited rights. I don't mean for this to be a distraction. I'm hoping this is gonna ward off distractions. And if, incidentally, there's any kid out there who's struggling with his identity, I hope this sends a message that it's okay. They can follow their dream, no matter what. Any young man, creed, whatever, can go out there and become a ballplayer. Or an interior decorator. *(He smiles beguilingly.)*

KIPPY. *(To us.)* And that was the beginning, sort of. *(The clubhouse. Kippy and Darren.)*

DARREN. Does this seem to you a Tuesday like any other, Kippy?

KIPPY. Well, Dar, you sort of gave it a different *tinge,* you gotta admit.

DARREN. I'm sensing a difference between the public and private realms.

KIPPY. How's that?

DARREN. Between the love and support depicted before the media and the slight *edging away* as from a bad smell, in the clubhouse.

KIPPY. You gotta expect that at first. It's the "Billy Bud" thing, Dar.

DARREN. Couldn't find the Cliff Notes for that one, Kippy.

KIPPY. This suddenly disturbing presence in a situation of men.

DARREN. I don't want to fuck any of you.

KIPPY. It's not about that, Darren. It's about *us* wanting to fuck you. *(Beat.)*

DARREN. Do you?

KIPPY. No. But as an amateur of social psychology? I suspect that we suspect that you suspect we do.

DARREN. Because that's presumed to be the presumption of my sudden peer group? That there are two classes of men: gay and in-denial?

KIPPY. Exactly.

DARREN. But I don't think that.

KIPPY. You don't?

DARREN. No.

KIPPY. Why not?

DARREN. Because lookin' around this clubhouse? I don't see a hotbed of suppressed sexual desire. In fact, I think this organization is lousy with latent *a*-sexuals.

KIPPY. Now how did you *draw* this conclusion?

DARREN. Because as an amateur of *nar*cissism I assume everybody in the world is just a version of me.

KIPPY. You?

DARREN. If I'm gonna have sex — and I *am* because I'm young and rich and famous and talented and handsome so it's a *law* — I'd rather do it with a guy, but when all is said and done, Kippy? I'd rather just play ball.

KIPPY. ... *I* am a passionate man, Darren.

DARREN. You're an intelligent man.

KIPPY. No, that's my reputation. But I'm not a naturally intelligent man.

DARREN. I'm afraid you are, Kippy.

KIPPY. No, I *look* like an intelligent man. That's always been true. Because my father and my brothers were these giant, hulking ... *Swedes*. Next to them I looked ... cerebral. Finally, I couldn't take the distance between my face and my essence, so I applied myself. Brought the two in line. Which is why *now* I'm —

DARREN. The most intelligent man in major-league baseball.

KIPPY. Well maybe not the *most* —

DARREN. Well, maybe not.

KIPPY. *(A hitch; then.)* ... *But what I'm saying is:* I *am* a passionate man. I mean, it's not a mutually exclusive proposition.

DARREN. You're a cauldron, Kippy.

KIPPY. I am that, Darren. You are too.

DARREN. I don't know 'bout that —

KIPPY. Well, now we'll find out. *(Martinez and Rodriguez pass by.)*

DARREN. Hey. *(Martinez and Rodriguez grunt something, exit.)* See, now that wasn't all that hospitable.

KIPPY. Well, you gotta give guys a chance to adjust, Dar. This was pretty much out of the blue — not as if anybody had a whole lotta prep time. A ten-minute team meeting and then BAM: The Media —

DARREN. I thought it was the easiest way to —

KIPPY. You didn't *tell* anybody, Dar.

DARREN. No.

KIPPY. Nobody was told ... *I* wasn't told.

DARREN. ... No. *(Beat.)*

KIPPY. Who did you tell?

DARREN. Well, like a half-hour before the reporters, *Skip.* *(Skipper appears.)*

KIPPY. And how did he —

DARREN. Ah, he was *Skip,* he was great —

KIPPY. *(To us.)* As he would be.

SKIPPER. This changes nothing, Darren.

KIPPY. Our manager is famed for his personal skills — toughness tempered by generosity — a wisdom that has more than once been referred to as "Solomonic."

SKIPPER. Absolutely nothing.

KIPPY. And he loves Darren.

SKIPPER. I *mean* that. *(He starts off.)*

KIPPY. Of course everybody loves Darren but with the Skipper it's different. He thinks he *invented* Darren. *(Beat.)*

DARREN. I didn't leave you out, Kippy.

KIPPY. ... Huh?

DARREN. I made the decision, you know, and then I *did* it. It didn't seem to require discussion, it wasn't anything extraordinary. It just seemed natural.

KIPPY. That's fantastic, Darren, that's so *great.*

DARREN. Okay.

KIPPY. ... So ... who is he? *(Beat.)*

DARREN. ... Who is ... *who?*

KIPPY. The guy. *(Darren looks puzzled.)* Your *guy.*

DARREN. ... I don't have a guy, Kippy.

KIPPY. ... But —

DARREN. No, Kippy, that wasn't what this is about. I'm not doin' this so I can *foist* some new couple on the world.

KIPPY. ... Oh.

DARREN. I mean, there've been *guys*. But it's not like there's some *guy*. Some ... significant *other*. Does this disappoint you?

KIPPY. No ... no ... Well. I had this idea about you and this *guy* and me and Susan and the three kids having dinner —

DARREN. Oh, so you had this sorta neo-comfy image floatin' through your head, I see. Kinduva Hallmark card with sodomy ... Sorry. Not happenin' ... Maybe someday.

KIPPY. Yea. Maybe someday. Maybe!

DARREN. ... Kippy, this seems to be a bigger event in *your* life than it is in mine.

KIPPY. I'm just so happy for you, Darren.

DARREN. Why?

KIPPY. Because now *you're* gonna be happy.

DARREN. I've always *been* happy.

KIPPY. But now you'll be *completely* happy. You've *named* yourself, Darren — you've put yourself into *words* — which means you're free in a way you've never been before.

DARREN. *(Half smile, touched but not quite getting it.)* ... Okay.

KIPPY. Of course there'll be the inevitable difficult period but —

DARREN. I don't think that.

KIPPY. — that's just — what?

DARREN. I don't think there's gonna be much of a difficult period.

KIPPY. ... Well, there's inevitably a difficult —

DARREN. Maybe if it were somebody else, but I don't see it. The sorta stuff that's goin' on with the guys now, but I don't take note of that, I can just ride above that.

KIPPY. ... Either way ... I'm really proud of you, Darren. Your future ... it's ... incredible to contemplate! *(With some diffidence, Jason approaches them.)*

JASON. Uh-h-h ... Darren?

DARREN. Yeah?

JASON. Jason? Chenier?

DARREN. Yeah, I recognize you.

JASON. ... Oh!

DARREN. You're our catcher.

JASON. Uh-huh.

DARREN. I got these really penetratin' eyes. I can see you from

13

alla way out there in center field.

JASON. Oh.

DARREN. Do *you* recognize this guy, Kippy?

KIPPY. Oh, yeah. But then, I'm at short, so I get a closer look.

JASON. So — u-h-h-h — I never made the first — u-h-h-h — approach to you — first — before — 'cause'a' who you were and who I'm not? But now — I *can* — and —

DARREN. Why is that? *(Beat.)*

JASON. Huh?

DARREN. Why is that? Why is it that now you can? *(Pause.)*

JASON. *(Mortified.)* Oh. Well, uh.

DARREN. *(Saves him.)* So you came to us, what, three weeks ago?

JASON. Oh! About three weeks, yeah. Three weeks. Almost three weeks and a *day* now —

KIPPY. From Asheville, was it?

JASON. Yeah, yeah, Triple-A Asheville.

DARREN. Ah-huh.

JASON. Up from Asheville.

DARREN. Well, that'd be the only direction.

JASON. Hey — yeah — huh?

DARREN. Huh what?

JASON. I didn't catch that.

DARREN. That's all right — you're bound to catch somethin' eventually —

JASON. *(Suddenly, to Darren.)* I'm in awe of you! *(Beat.)*

DARREN. Okay.

JASON. I'm in *awe* of you —

DARREN. Sure —

JASON. And I just wanna say: the whole gay thing — doesn't mean — I don't — it doesn't. I'm in awe.

DARREN. Yeah, okay.

JASON. I know this guy that read a book once?

KIPPY. No!

JASON. Oh yeah. It was about Grecians. The book.

DARREN. ... Grecians?

JASON. The Greek people from ... Greece.

DARREN. Oh. Oh!

JASON. From long ago.

DARREN. *Ah*-huh. Does this story seem to be heading someplace fishy to you, Kippy?

KIPPY. No, this story seems to be heading *away* from someplace

14

fishy to me, Dar.

JASON. Anyway, those Greeks … they … *(i.e.: were big faggots.)* And they created … *(He makes a big circular gesture with his arms to indicate "civilization and stuff.")* They made … the pyramids.

DARREN. *They* made the pyramids? The Greeks did?

JASON. Oh, yeah.

DARREN. Whaddya know? Whad the Egyptians make, Kippy?

KIPPY. *Funny Girl. (Darren gives him a look.)* Well, Omar Sharif …

JASON. All I'm saying. *(He gives them a confirmatory nod. Exits. Darren looks at Kippy.)*

KIPPY. There's gonna be a lotta shit like that. *(Lights. To us:)* There was a lotta shit like that … *(Lockers. Darren undresses after a game. Toddy comes out of the shower, just a towel draped around his waist. He takes off the towel, starts drying his hair.)*

DARREN. *(Casually.)* Hey.

TODDY. Okay, so now I gotta be worrying about this?

DARREN. About what is that, Toddy?

TODDY. So now I gotta go around worrying that every time I'm naked or dressed or whatever you're checking out my ass.

DARREN. I'm not facing your ass at the moment, Toddy.

TODDY. Like *that.* Not just skeevous glances, I gotta put up with lewd remarks.

DARREN. That wasn't lewd, Toddy.

TODDY. You're not *getting* me, man. Why do I have to go around this room, which is, has been, which is this sancchewy, rackled with self-consciousness about my body?

DARREN. Are you rackled, Toddy?

TODDY. I am, I am *rackled,* man.

DARREN. Why'n't ya work out more?

TODDY. What?

DARREN. I said: Why'n't you get dressed, then?

TODDY. Huh?

DARREN. I said: WHY DON'T YOU COVER YOURSELF? You're the one's all shakin' out here like pom-poms — it's not, you know, nudity's not *required* here, Toddy. *(Toddy, rackled by this, wraps a towel around his waist.)*

TODDY. You're not *gettin'* me, man. Why should I *have* to get dressed? Why should I have to cover myself *ever?*

DARREN. Well, 'cause if you have some hope of reentering decent society, they make ya. They *insist* on it. *(Beat.)*

TODDY. … Ya wanna know your problem, Darren?

15

DARREN. Wha'sat, Toddy?

TODDY. You have been damaged by your aura of invincible. You think because you're all this talented or whatever that nothing's gonna get at ya.

DARREN. That's pretty right.

TODDY. But the thing, Darren? An' I know nobody says this stuff to you 'cause'a' your salary leadership an' shit, the thing? You're *not*.

DARREN. I think I am.

TODDY. You know who doesn't agree? God.

DARREN. God. Wow. Heavy.

TODDY. God can *kill* ya, man.

DARREN. God's gonna kill us all, Toddy.

TODDY. God doesn't spare ballplayers, man.

DARREN. Nope.

TODDY. Not even All Stars. Not even Hall of *Famers*. God got Clemente. God got *Munson*.

DARREN. That's right. That's right, he did.

TODDY. Gehrig, man. Gehrig's got a *fate* named after him.

DARREN. "A fate." Wow. I didn't know you could talk like that, Toddy. Ya got a real sorta poetry of the ignoramus goin' on, don't ya?

TODDY. I'm making a *point* here, man. God can get ya.

DARREN. That's true, Toddy. That's very true. God can get me. But short'a' God, there's nobody … *(Toddy is rackled by this. Darren's got the last of his clothes off and is reaching for a towel.)*

TODDY. Now what the hell is *that*?

DARREN. Aw, you know what *that* is, Toddy. Why're ya lookin' at it's the question.

TODDY. What is the *thinking* behind that move, man? Why did you *do* that?

DARREN. *(Wrapping towel around his waist.)* I'm takin' a shower, Toddy.

TODDY. See? That's my point, man. That's my point.

DARREN. Toddy, this is beneath you.

TODDY. Nothing is beneath me, Darren.

DARREN. Be that as it may; as an enlightened individual —

TODDY. "Enlightened," "Enlightened"! I know that word —

DARREN. You *do*? That makes like, what, *seven*?

TODDY. Enlightened is like this thing, idea, where all standards go to hell, and like, decency, and shit. I am *not* enlightened, Darren. I *pride* myself on that.

DARREN. Well in that case, let me enlighten you about one thing

16

— My sexuality is not your problem —

TODDY. It is — it is —

DARREN. Naw, Toddy, uh-uh. If it concerns you, it's only 'cause as of yet, it hasn't diminished me to any noticeable extent. I'm still *me*. I'm still the man. What actually confounds you is somethin' else.

TODDY. Okay, so now, in addition to everything else, you're in charge of all meaning?

DARREN. Oh yeah, oh yeah.

TODDY. That's very interesting, Darren; that's very interesting to know. Who made you God?

DARREN. God made me God, Toddy. Or at least invested me with God-like attributes. Whereas you? *(Pause.)* Are not God. You are a dimwit.

TODDY. I'm not a dimwit, Darren.

DARREN. Did you know your name is a verb? … Yeah, it started in that playoff game last year, do you remember this? When you thought that fly ball you caught was the third out so 'stead of throwin' it, you *handed* it to that slutty-lookin' girl in the front row while meanwhile seven, eight guys crossed home plate —

TODDY. Two guys, *two guys* —

DARREN. Yeah; it was the only time the offense and the defense ever scored simultaneously. That's when the verb "to Koovitz" got coined. It means "to focus on the wrong thing."

TODDY. … I march to a different drummer.

DARREN. And sometimes you halt in the middle'a' the parade. I don't do that.
I never halt.
That's why I'm better'n'you.

TODDY. But you're queer.

DARREN. And I'm better at that than you, too. *(Lights. Kippy, solo.)*

KIPPY. So the question was: *Why?*
Or why *now?*
Because, strangely enough, Darren wasn't on the verge of being outed. There weren't even any rumors … that I knew of.
He was too discreet. Or maybe he really did have as little libido as he claims.
Hard to say.
It's possible he just got tired of paying those courtesy calls on the famous girlfriends he'd cultivated for a while.
I don't know.
We were best friends, but …

I started to think it had something to do with the last time he'd seen Davey.

Davey Battle.

Who back then was known to be and later became world-famous as Dar's best friend.

From — Jeez — forever.

It was after they got together that I noticed his *mood* started changing, things started to seem to *shift* in him.

One night, we were playing Davey's team, we destroyed them, actually, and after the game Davey and Darren went out together. This was one week before the big announcement. *(A lounge. Darren and Davey Battle.)*

DARREN. So okay, this is not a bad place.

DAVEY. I'm not about to be goin' with you to bad places, my man.

DARREN. By which I mean this is not a *good* place. I mean we're not at Serendipity, scarfin' down root-beer floats.

DAVEY. Shit, no.

DARREN. 'Cause I'm always wonderin' with you, Bats — I'm always wonderin' — "When's he finally gonna go over the edge? When's his idea of *fun* gonna be *square* dancin' at the First Methodist Church?"

DAVEY. Shit, no.

DARREN. So tell me: You'll say "shit."

DAVEY. I *will* say "shit."

DARREN. And you'll say "fuck."

DAVEY. If provoked, I will say "fuck."

DARREN. But you won't say "goddamnit."

DAVEY. I will not, and I wish you wouldn't either.

DARREN. So how's Linda?

DAVEY. Linda is excellent, thank you.

DARREN. And Tadana and Tahica and Davey Junior?

DAVEY. They're very fine.

DARREN. Why is it that all ballplayers have three kids?

DAVEY. Baseball is a game of threes. Multiples of three. Three strikes. Nine innings. Nine players (except in the debased American League). Now I'm not into numerology, which is a heathen practice, but baseball is a game of threes. Where are *your* three?

DARREN. I'm hitting three-thirty-three. I'm on course for thirty-three stolen bases —

DAVEY. You deflect me, my man.

DARREN. Yeah, well, sometimes I do.

DAVEY. Why? *Why* do you?

DARREN. *(Deflecting him.)* Do you want that beer?

DAVEY. You've got your own.

DARREN. That's not the issue — do you *want* that beer?

DAVEY. I ordered it, didn't I?

DARREN. Yeah, but you sure you wouldn't prefer a nice herb tea?

DAVEY. … A nice herb tea would be nice.

DARREN. But you can't have it, 'cause, in addition to bein' a *good man,* you need to have it known that you're a *regular guy.* I mean, we're not here to shoot the shit, we're here to publicize how well-rounded you are.

DAVEY. You got a problem with how well-rounded I am, Darren?

DARREN. Nah, Bats, no problem. You're just funny, that's all.

DAVEY. "Funny."

Huh!

I'm going to tell you something that's going to surprise you, Darren: You are probably a happier man in your career than I am in mine.

DARREN. That so?

DAVEY. That is so. Well, look at tonight: I played a better game than you, but your team won. Why is that would you say?

DARREN. We're a better team.

DAVEY. That's the truth. And this points up the difference between our superstardoms. Our talents are similar, but yours are muted because you're on a superior team. Whereas on my team of stumblebums, I'm an aberration. My achievements are solitary — which creates a certain loneliness — which is why you're a happier man in your career.

DARREN. I'm sorry you feel that way.

DAVEY. But I'm a happier man in my *life.*

And do you know why *that* is?

DARREN. I'm afraid to ask —

DAVEY. Because I am *well-rounded.*

Because I have my wife.

I have my three.

Where are your three, Darren?

DARREN. I don't have my three, Bats. I don't even want them, no offense to your superior domestic arrangements.

DAVEY. Who do you love, Darren? *(Hesitation.)* No, now I know that's a difficult question, I know that's not the sort 'a' thing men talk to each other about, but we've got to, 'cause we're close and it's

19

important.

DARREN. I don't love anybody, Bats. *(Beat.)* My parents. *(Beat.)* I *like* a lot of people.

DAVEY. That's a situation you're gonna have to change, Darren. Because until you love somebody ... Ohh — you're all sly, all quick-witted and mysterious — this is your aura. Polite but mischievous, that's your charm. But until you love somebody, do you understand what I'm saying? You'll never know your true nature.

DARREN. I know my true nature.

DAVEY. I do too, Darren, and it is *good.*

DARREN. Do you think it's good, Bats? Do you think you like me?

DAVEY. I *know I* like you, Darren. You're my friend.

But now you're seen As Through a Glass Darkly.

Do you know what I'm saying to you?

I drink my one beer, and I cuss my two cuss words loudly, so as to manifest my true nature.

I want my whole self known.

You too, Darren. You should, too. *(Lights. Mason Marzac, solo.)*

MASON. And a couple of weeks earlier I would have barely recognized the name! Then the announcement — that incredible act of elective heroism — and it was as if I'd known him my whole life — as if he'd been something latent in my subconscious.

A lot of people felt that way.

And we all knew everything in an instant — all his contradictions — his white father, his black mother; he was universally beloved, he was a little remote — and now the biggest contradiction of all — But the contradictions all seemed reconciled in him; that was his genius.

Often, in interviews, he'd be asked: Do you consider yourself black or white?

And he'd reply, "I'm black *and* white."

As if that were the only answer possible. As if no sane person could have a problem with that. And *now* I was to handle his money, which is a really intimate thing, and we were meeting for the first time and I thought, God, just let me contain myself — *(Lights. Darren joins Mason.)* Mr. Lemming — Mason Marzac: a pleasure to meet you!

DARREN. *(Shakes hand.)* Nice to meet you.

MASON. Yes; a very great pleasure —

DARREN. Great —

MASON. Very great in*deed.*

DARREN. … Okay.

MASON. … The purpose of this meeting is largely just to get acquainted, although —

DARREN. Nothing's happened to my money?

MASON. Uum, nothing you wouldn't *want* to.

DARREN. 'Cause this is a time in my life when things are shifting a little and my money's one'a the solid —

MASON. *(Overlapped.)* Yes, I'd say — I'd *say* they're shifting —

DARREN. … Meaning?

MASON. Oh. Oh, nothing … You know, a funny thing. I saw your commercial last night — for the first time ever. The one for the marshmallow spread?

DARREN. Oh yeah? When was that?

MASON. Last night, well, around two in the morning.

DARREN. Whereabouts do you live?

MASON. Chelsea.

DARREN. Yeah, that's where my spot runs these days — Chelsea at around two in the morning. Ya see, there's some concern that people might question what it is I'm doing with that marshmallow spread —

MASON. — whereas in Chelsea after midnight, it's a question that delights! *(Instantly regrets it.)*

DARREN. … Something like that, yeah.
So why are you my guy, now? What happened to Abe?

MASON. Arthritis, sclerosis, Florida. In other words: retirement. Didn't you get the letter?

DARREN. I don't really read my mail.

MASON. Assistants to assist with the work caused by assistants, hm?

DARREN. So you've taken over Abe's clients.

MASON. Oh — God — no — not *all* — I am in fact largely … *yours.*

DARREN. … I guess I got *you* because the guys with families are too distracted.

MASON. Interesting inference but *no.* Recently it's been noticed that I have taken some clients with fairly modest portfolios and made them *rather* wealthy.

DARREN. What kind of clients were those?

MASON. Oh, you know — *models.* Not even supermodels. The kind that go to restaurants and are barely snide. Now they can retire. I'm sort of the Rookie of the Year, after a fashion. In my own little world, I'm you! *(Silence. Mason blanches.)* Oh dear God, forgive me. I didn't mean to sug*gest* —

DARREN. Nah, it's okay —

MASON. It didn't occur to me —

DARREN. Not a problem —

MASON. — that by saying "I'm you," I'm implying you're me — I would never — *(Darren puts a comforting hand over Mason's clenched hands.)*

DARREN. Ss-sh. *(Mason gets quiet.)*

MASON. Thank you, you're very generous. Well, uh — Last time you and Abe spoke —

DARREN. We didn't speak —

MASON. Oh?

DARREN. I think he spoke to my agent.

MASON. Oh, really.

DARREN. I'm not sure; I don't really speak to my agent.

MASON. Oh — well —

DARREN. You're gonna have to ask my assistant.

MASON. And how would I reach *him?*

DARREN. I don't know, ya know, I hardly ever see him.

MASON. Then with whom are you in touch?

DARREN. Only the Lord, Mason; only the Lord. *(Beat.)* Nah, I'm just goofin' on ya. So what was it that Abe and "I" discussed?

MASON. Well — according to Abe's instructions — you said — or, rather, someone speaking for you said you wanted — that is, some courier of your desire sug*gest*ed that it might be a good idea to take up a conspicuous charity of some sort.

DARREN. Oh. *(Beat.)* And why'd I wanna do that?

MASON. Because it's a good, a very good idea.

DARREN. Why?

MASON. Oh! Well … there's a feeling that when money … is too densely concentrated … I mean, when one person has too much of it … there's a feeling that it's … damaging.

DARREN. To who?

MASON. To the … well, to the economy as a whole. The body politic … To goodness. *(He gives a quiet little laugh. Beat.)*

DARREN. We're only talking a hundred-six mil here. I mean it's not like some *vast sum.* Amortized or whatever over six years. *(Beat.)*

MASON. On the other hand, it's not *not* a vast sum. *(Beat.)*

DARREN. The thing that worries me is: this. Ya know how every now an' then, people — not *people* but, for instance, *business* managers, 'round about Christmas, instead of sendin' you a nice cut-glass bowl, will inform you that in lieu of an actual present a donation has been made in your name to The Such-And-Such Foundation, dedicated to the cause of fightin' … This-And-That. Do you understand what I'm sayin'? 'Stead of another meaningless, pretty *objet,* they're givin' you the gift of phony concern. I don't want that. 'f' I do some big charitable thing, I want it to be somethin' I give a shit about.

MASON. Absolutely. *(Beat.)* So what do you give a shit about? *(Pause. Longer pause.)*

DARREN. Let me get back to ya on that one.

MASON. Uh —

DARREN. Okay — okay — set up some kinda foundation.

MASON. Excellent. To benefit whom?

DARREN. … Aw fuck me.

MASON. The question needs to be asked.

DARREN. Make it kids.

MASON. … Good …

DARREN. Kids'a' some kind … fucked-up kids. Some kinda fucked-up kids. Little kids!

MASON. That will be superb.

DARREN. Fucked-up kids under ten.

MASON. Splendid.

DARREN. … Gay kids. *(Beat.)*

MASON. Gay kids … under ten?

DARREN. Yeah. *(Beat.)*

MASON. We *could* do that. I can foresee some problems in qualifications testing.

DARREN. Hey, Mason?

MASON. Yes?

DARREN. I'm goofin' on ya, again. *(Hesitation.)*

MASON. Ah.

DARREN. I've got some concerns but I'm just havin' some trouble *synthesizin'* them for the moment.

MASON. *(Bold, in a rush.)* I want to say what you've done is a very wonderful thing for the community.

DARREN. What community would that be? *(Beat.)*

MASON. Well, *our* community. Of course, I don't really *have* a community. Or, more precisely, the community won't really have me. And I don't like communities, in general. I avoid them. I'm outside them. *(Beat.)* Possibly beneath them.

DARREN. I don't really have a community, either. I'm above them.

MASON. Well, then, you've done a very wonderful thing for a community to which neither of us belongs but with which we will both, inevitably, be associated.

DARREN. Oh. That wasn't why I did it.

MASON. Even so, it was tremendously brave.

DARREN. It's only brave if ya think somethin' *bad*'s gonna happen. They don't ... to me.

MASON. ... Never?

DARREN. Pretty much.

MASON. Why is that?

DARREN. Because I'm in baseball. And so is God, Mason. So is God.

MASON. That's more-or-less your all-purpose punch line, isn't it?

DARREN. No, I *mean* it this time. Look around you: Typhoons, earthquakes, avalanches. War. He's absent. The Holocaust. Nowhere. That's not how He works. He's got a whimsical nature. He makes Himself known in stupid stuff. Trivia. Baseball. The Grammys. But especially baseball.

MASON. *(Half-tantalized.)* ... I've been watching some baseball ... lately.

DARREN. Zat so?

MASON. It seems ... remarkably interesting. Especially the numbers.

DARREN. The numbers, huh?

MASON. Yes — that guy who hit sixty-one home runs to tie the guy who hit sixty-one home runs in nineteen-sixty-one and did it on his father's sixty-first birthday. That's ...

DARREN. Oh, yeah. There's a lot of that. Keep watchin'. You'll see. *(Mason smiles tentatively.)* So my money's okay?

MASON. Flourishing.

DARREN. Well, that's gotta be a sign, too, right? *(Lights. Kippy, solo.)*

KIPPY. Except that then, all of a sudden, we started losing ... bad. Apparently, our pitching staff held a secret meeting at which they voted to slump in unison. Take our Ace for example: Takeshi Kawabata-*san.* *(Kawabata appears, pitching.)* Acquired in the off-season from the Fukuoka Daieh Hawks, Kawabata came with a dazzling arsenal of pitches, a breathtaking contract, and a truly stupendous lack of English language skills, which, at times, seemed willful. For the first half of the season, he pitched brilliantly. He was *still* pitching brilliantly — for about six innings a start. Then the seventh would come, where he would break down completely, and leave the game ... *(Kawabata breaks down, leaves the game.)* ... ashamed, disgraced, and basically inconsolable because, speaking no English, he never spoke at all, and was alone in his defeat. *(Kawabata's gone.)* Then we'd go to our bullpen guys who'd all begun to grip the ball like it was some chunk of alien matter that had fallen from the sky, and alluva sudden we're in first place by only half-a-game.

But we're the Empires — we fix these situations.

Word came back from Double A Utica about a guy who was burning up the place — with an E.R.A. under *one* over nineteen games. And He Came Unto Us. *(Shane Mungitt appears. He throws a series of pitches. But he throws like a dybbuk. And he keeps throwing.)* And we were winners again.

Which was how things were supposed to be.

But he spoke less English than the Japanese guy.

And there was something worse than that:

He didn't seem to like the game.

Now, over the course of a hundred-sixty-two games, guys are gonna be angry, smelly, turbulent, fractious, but just drop a key word or two and most of them are all of a sudden going to remember being four — and dad and the Wiffle ball and it's *too much emotion.*

Which is appropriate.

Almost everybody picks up on that almost right away. *(Lights. Mason, solo.)*

MASON. So I've done what was suggested. I continued to watch and I have come (with no little excitement) to understand that baseball is a perfect metaphor for hope in a Democratic society.

It has to do with the rules of play.

It has to do with the mode of enforcement of these rules.

It has to do with certain nuances and grace notes of the game.

First, it's the remarkable symmetry of everything.

All those threes and multiples of three — calling attention to — virtually making a *fetish* of the game's noble equality.

Equality, that is, of opportunity.

Everyone is given exactly the same chance.

And the opportunity to exercise that chance at his own pace.

There's none of that scurry, none of that relentlessness that marks other games — basketball, football, hockey.

I've never watched basketball, football, or hockey, but I'm sure I wouldn't like them. Or maybe I would, but it wouldn't be the same.

What I mean is, in baseball there's no clock.

What could be more generous than to give everyone all these opportunities and the time to seize them in, as well? And with each turn at the plate, there's the possibility of turning the situation to your favor. Down to the very last try.

And then, to insure that everything remains fair, justices are ranged around the park to witness and assess the play.

And if the justice errs, an appeal can be made.

It's invariably turned down, but that's part of what makes the metaphor so right.

Because even in the most well-meant of systems, error is inevitable. Even within the fairest of paradigms, unfairness will creep in.

And baseball is better than Democracy — or at least than Democracy as it's practiced in this country — because unlike Democracy, baseball acknowledges loss.

While conservatives tell you, leave things alone and no one will lose, and liberals tell you, interfere a lot and no one will lose, baseball says: Someone will lose. Not only *says* it — insists upon it!

So that baseball achieves the tragic vision that Democracy evades. Evades *and* embodies.

Democracy is lovely, but baseball's more mature. *(Pause.)* Another thing I like is the home-run trot.

Not the mad dash around the bases when it's an inside-the-ballpark home run — I'm not sure I've ever *seen* an inside-the-ballpark home run — I'm talking about that graceful little canter when the ball has been crushed, and it's missing, and the outcome's not in doubt.

What I like about it is it's so unnecessary.

The ball's gone, no one's going to bring it back. And can anyone doubt that a man capable of launching a ball four-hundred feet is somehow going to *fail* to touch a base when he's running uninterfered-with?

For all intents and purposes, the game, at that moment, is not being played.

If duration-of-game is an issue — and I'm given to believe that duration-of-game *is* an issue — the sensible thing would be to say, yes, that's gone, add a point to the score, and send the next batter to the plate.

But that's not what happens.

Instead, play is suspended for a celebration.

A man rounds four bases and, if he's with the home team, the crowd has a catharsis.

And from the way he runs, you learn something about the man.

And from the way they cheer, you learn something about the crowd. And I like this because I don't believe in God.

Or — well — don't *know* about God. Or about any of that … metaphysical murk.

Yet, I like to believe that something about being human is … good. And I think what's best about us is manifested in our desire to show respect for one another. For what we can be. *(Darren enters, carrying bat.)* And that's what we do in our ceremonies, isn't it? Honor ourselves as we pass through Time?

And it seems to me that to conduct this ceremony not before a game or after a game but in the very *heart* of a game is … quite … well, does any other game do that?

That's baseball. *(Beat. Darren takes his excellent batting stance. Signals to someone located audience-ward to throw a ball. He swings. The swing is beautiful. It connects, there's that lovely sound. Darren and Mason watch the ball soar. A moment.)*

DARREN. *(Casually.)* Baseball.

MASON. *(Happily.)* Yes.

That is, too. *(Lights. Kippy enters.)*

KIPPY. *(As if interrupted.)* As I was saying:

We kept on winning and the new guy was a machine —

But we had no idea who he was.

And it got so, eventually, we wanted to introduce ourselves. *(The Clubhouse. Kippy, Darren, some of the others. Mungitt alone.)*

KIPPY. So, uh, Shane? *(Shane looks up. Some of the other guys do, too. You get the sense that maybe this is the first time anyone's spoken to him. He says nothing.)* Now *you* say *hello. (Beat.)*

SHANE. Hey.

KIPPY. Darren here and I — we've been wondering something. *(Beat.)*

SHANE. Whuzzat?

KIPPY. Well … we're wondering who you *are,* Shane. *(Beat.)*

SHANE. Oh?

KIPPY. You never introduced yourself.

DARREN. That's a violation of protocol.

KIPPY. Generally, the new guys introduce themselves to the old guys. Not the other way around.

SHANE. Oh.

KIPPY. You don't expect, do you, the great Darren Lemming to search out every two-bit whatchamadoo from A-ball Bumfuck, do you?

SHANE. Uuuhh … sorry. *(Beat.)*

KIPPY. Well, that's all right.

DARREN. So who are ya, Shane?

SHANE. I'm Shane Mungitt. *(Beat.)*

KIPPY. I think we'd like to delve a little deeper, if we might. 'Cause you've come into our clubhouse —

DARREN. Scared the shit outta everybody —

KIPPY. With your —

DARREN. — general —

KIPPY. — *fast* ball — and we'd like to make you a little more comprehensible to ourselves —

DARREN. We'd like some information —

KIPPY. Some of the basics. Okay? *(Beat.)*

SHANE. 'kay.

KIPPY. Where do you come from, Shane?

SHANE. … Double A.

KIPPY. No, that's not — that's not what I —

SHANE. Double A *U*tica —

KIPPY. That's not what I meant. *(Beat.)*

SHANE. Oh. *(Beat.)*

KIPPY. Where were you *born?*

SHANE. Oh! Arkansas.

KIPPY. Oh, Arkansas, now we know something —

SHANE. Arkansas … Tennessee …

KIPPY. Arkansas … Tennessee …

SHANE. One'a them. *(Beat.)* Mississippi.

KIPPY. Okay, let me try an easier one. Where'd you grow up, mostly, Shane?

SHANE. … Lotta places.

DARREN. But *mostly? (Beat.)*

SHANE. This sorta group home. *(Beat.)*

KIPPY. Group home?

SHANE. Uh-huh, yeah.

KIPPY. Like a commune?

DARREN. A kibbutz?

SHANE. Nah.

KIPPY. Hippie stuff? Are we talking hippie stuff, Shane?

SHANE. Nah.

DARREN. Then what then?

SHANE. Well, it was … u-u-u-u-h-h … orphanage. *(Beat.)*

DARREN. They still have those? Orphanages?

28

SHANE. Kinda.

KIPPY. You an orphan, Shane?

SHANE. Oh, yeah. *(Beat.)*

KIPPY. I'm very sorry to hear that.

DARREN. Didn't you ever go to foster homes or something like that?

SHANE. Oh, yeah. But u-u-h-h ... I got ... they returned me.

KIPPY. Returned? Why was that?

DARREN. Were you already offensive as a youth, Shane?

SHANE. U-u-h ... Maybe ... Nah, I think it was more like 'cause'a' the way I became an orphan.

KIPPY. What way was that?

SHANE. This murder-suicide ... attempt?

DARREN. Murder-suicide *attempt?*

SHANE. ... Successful.

KIPPY. ... Oh.

DARREN. ... Oh.

SHANE. My dad, see? Shot my mom? Then turned the gun on himself? The foster people didn't like that story. They u-u-u-h-h ...

KIPPY. Why'd he do that, your dad?

SHANE. U-u-h-h. I can't say. I was only ... fourteen months at the time ... But I met this guy? Later? Who knew 'em? And he said they didn't get along that well.

KIPPY. I bet that was it!

SHANE. Yeah —

DARREN. That *musta* been it.

SHANE. Yeah. *(Beat.)* Sometimes I think I can remember it.

KIPPY. The —

SHANE. The ... u-u-h-h ... killings. Sometimes I think I can see it.

KIPPY. Well, that happens sometimes, Shane. You hear a story enough and it becomes so vivid in your imagination you think you were there. *(Beat.)*

SHANE. I was there. *(Beat.)*

KIPPY. What?

SHANE. For ... 'bout ... three days.

I was all — they found me —

I was all bawling — and dehydrate.

Shitted all over myself.

That's how they found me.

Sometimes I think I remember it.

Think I see it. *(Beat. He starts to laugh, a loose, quietly crazy sound.)*

KIPPY. Was that a lie, Shane? Was that whole story something you *made up?*

SHANE. *(Surprised.)* No.

DARREN. Then what are you laughing for?

SHANE. ... Whut's not funny? *(He looks at them contemptuously, walks off.)*

TODDY. *(From the background.)* What an asshole. *(Lights.)*

KIPPY. *(Kippy, solo.)* I, of course, didn't think so.

I thought: He just can't talk.

He doesn't know any words.

And that's always seemed to me the worst kind of hardship: not to have words to name the world with ... to shape yourself to ...

So, while most of the guys hated him and kept their distance, I secretly, fell hopelessly in ... custody of him.

I decided he was my responsibility.

Because I understood him. And no one else did.

So ... he kept on closing.

And we kept on winning. *(Guys do victory stuff.)* And he was this phenom, this sensation. Everybody wanted to talk to him.

And one night all the words he didn't know, he said.

On television. *(The team ranges around, as though watching TV. Shane appears, solo.)*

TV VOICE. And so what is it like for you, Shane, a young kid out of nowhere, pitching for Double A Utica, to be brought up by the defending world champions when they're starting to struggle a bit, and to come in and, essentially, save their season?

KIPPY. And he replied:

SHANE. Well, I tell ya, it's a pretty humblin' thing.

I'm just this kid outta nowhere and alluva sudden — WHAM, I'm on this team.

An' it's a pretty funny team, ya know.

A pretty funny bunch'a' guys.

Now don't get me wrong.

I don't mind the colored people — the gooks an' the spics an' the coons an' like that.

But *every night* t'have'ta take a shower with a *faggot?*

Do ya know what I'm sayin'? *(Beat. Team watches in frozen horror.)*

Do ya *get* me? *(Hold. Fade out.)*

End of Act One

ACT TWO

Lights. William R. Danziger, solo.

WILLIAM R. DANZIGER. Dear Mr. Lemming:
I am writing you first to express my outrage at the appalling remarks made by Shane Mungitt, and to commend you on the grace you've shown through this whole difficult time, beginning with the brave and unprecedented revelation of your sexual preference.
You are, indeed, a sterling young man, and an example to all.
Mr. Lemming, I have an eight-year-old son. I would be proud if you were my son's chemistry teacher or math teacher or even — especially gym teacher.
If you were his religious instructor, I am sure you would imbue him with a truer sense of Christian charity than any of the questionable types holding forth in the Sunday school he now attends.
Were my son your age and gay — an option, being gay, that is — that he already knows is open to him since all we ask is that he follow the truth of his heart — he could do no better than find a man like you for his lover.
It would be a kick having you as a friend. And I would have no trouble sharing a communal shower with you after a round of tennis at whatever club.
But do you have to play BASEBALL?
Don't you know what baseball *means to me?*
I wish you well in all other things, but this hurts my feelings.
Cordially,
William R. Danziger
Rahway, New Jersey *(Lights. Kippy, towel wrapped around his waist, solo.)*
KIPPY. But mostly it was support. Which was killing Darren. *(Darren enters.)*
DARREN. I am so freakin' *sick* of this *welcome* I'm getting.
KIPPY. Welcome?
DARREN. Ever since fuckin' Mungitt went on TV.
Alluva sudden I'm a *victim. Fuck* that! I want slurs — brickbats —

31

epithets. Do you know what I'm *getting?*
KIPPY. What?
DARREN. Offers!
KIPPY. Like...?
DARREN. Endorsements for, like, cheap furniture.
KIPPY. Those can be very moving.
DARREN. *Fuck* this shit, Kippy.
Do you know what I'm *getting?*
KIPPY. ... Offers?
DARREN. Compassion. I need compassion?
KIPPY. Nah.
DARREN. Don't you have compassion for me, you *envy* me, this is how it is with me, this is how it's always been, take your fuckin' compassion an' stick it up your ass, 'cause you're not getting' *me* there!
KIPPY. *(Hugs him with compassion.)* I know how it is, man, and I *feel* for you.
DARREN. *(Throwing him off.)* You fuckin' faggot. *(Kippy laughs. Darren quiets down, gets somber.)* Ya know what it is, Kippy.
They think they've figured me out.
They think my secret's out.
And what's gonna follow is this cavalcade of revelation.
IS THAT WHAT EVERYBODY THINKS?
You think you're gonna get this *torrent* of *me* comin' at ya?
You think you *know* me? You think you know my *secret?*
Shit, that wasn't a secret — that was an omission. I've *got* a secret — but that's not it.
KIPPY. What is?
DARREN. ... Wha — ?
KIPPY. What is your secret? You said you have a secret.
DARREN. ... I don't *have* a secret, Kippy. I *am* a secret.
KIPPY. Even from me? *(A beat. The question slides away.)*
DARREN. I'm sick of baseball. I want out.
KIPPY. Oh, bullshit.
DARREN. I mean it — I might walk right out of all this —
KIPPY. Nobody playing the way you're playing "walks right out" of it — nobody making your salary "walks right out" of it —
DARREN. How do you know? What makes you sure'a' that?
KIPPY. The world's old, there've been a lot of people; I extrapolate.
DARREN. Maybe I'm somethin' that's never been seen before. Maybe I'm somethin' brand new. Maybe —

KIPPY. I *play* with you. I play on your team (which is not to say that I play on your team but) I ... play on your team.

I know you.

I know you when you're playing.

DARREN. ... Things are ... changing. I'm changing.

KIPPY. I like you better now.

DARREN. Bullshit.

KIPPY. No — I liked you before — *loved* you in a manly sort of way. But now you're ... more human.

DARREN. What was I before?

KIPPY. Sort of ... godly.

DARREN. And now I'm human?

KIPPY. Yeah.

DARREN. Kippy?

KIPPY. Yeah, Dar?

DARREN. Isn't that a *demotion? (Lights. Kippy, solo.)*

KIPPY. So, Shane was suspended for a period of time to-be-determined, and without Shane, we started losing again. But Darren didn't. Darren soared. Darren brought his average up to around four-hundred. Darren leapt tall walls in a single bound, robbed the opposing team of home runs routinely, led the league in ... everything. And after each game, he would quickly and silently shower, then quickly and silently leave. All of which led to some dark post-game conspiracy theories. *(The Showers. Toddy, Jason, Martinez, Rodriguez, Kawabata showering. Kippy hangs up towel, joins them.)*

TODDY. Fucker did this on purpose.

Fucker did this to make us look bad.

Fucker had the whole thing in mind the whole time.

KIPPY. What whole thing's that, Toddy?

TODDY. This is *it*, Kippy.

Darren's always felt this inferiority thing because his friend Davey Battle gets to be a showboat on a lousy team, see? And Darren, 'cause we're *good*, was thinkin', shit, people aren't watchin' *me* enough, people don't know it's *me* not the *team* so I'll do this thing.

KIPPY. And what thing is that?

TODDY. The thing — the thing — the thing that's happened!

KIPPY. Oh, I see. So his thinking went: I'll reveal myself to be a homosexual, whereupon a racist, homophobe, hillbilly will be brought up to close and then, on television, reveal a medley of reprehensible social attitudes leading to his suspension which will lead

33

in *turn* to a general team demoralization *from which* I alone will be exempt, *thereby* becoming what I have always longed to be: a solo hotshot on a mediocre club.

TODDY. ... Yeah.

KIPPY. Well, that sounds about right to me.

RODRIGUEZ. *Tico.*

MARTINEZ. *(Overlapping.) Di me lo.*

RODRIGUEZ. *¡¡Ven acá, de que cojones hablan esta gente?!*

MARTINEZ. *Coño yo ni se.*

RODRIGUEZ. *¿Tu crees que un dia hablaremos ese jodio idioma?*

MARTINEZ. *Completamente, espero que no. (Kawabata exits.)*

KIPPY. But I think what we've really got going, Toddy? Is even *subt*ler than your analysis. I think what's happened to us as a team — and what has not happened to Darren simply because he's better — is we're in a kind of mourning.

TODDY. Huh?

KIPPY. Very well-put. I think we've experienced a kind of profound loss. First in the physical realm — in the *sex*ual realm, even. *(Rodriguez and Martinez look sharply to Kippy, almost unison.)*

TODDY. *Huh?*

KIPPY. I take your point, *however.*

Well, look at us now.

How we turn from each other.

How when we turn *to* each other we maintain eye contact. *(Rodriguez and Martinez look away.)* Before, this wasn't necessary.

We were Men.

This meant we could be girlish.

We could pat fannies, snap towels; hug

Now ...

What do we do with our stray homosexual impulses?

JASON. Pardon?

KIPPY. Yes?

JASON. You were talking to me, right?

KIPPY. No, Jason, I wasn't. *(Beat.)*

JASON. Oh. *(Beat. He turns crimson. He exits.)*

KIPPY. You see?

We've lost a kind of paradise.

We see that we are naked.

TODDY. Bullshit. *(They leave showers, cross to lockers.)*

KIPPY. And our refuge? We have none.

We might want to assume a defensive hostility, an aggression. The

danger there is, we become Shane Mungitt. So our anger, our male-
ness, is lost to us. We're *tight.* We choke up on the bat. We play short
flies on the bounce. We suck. *(Shane Mungitt enters, in his civvies.)*
SHANE. U-u-u-h-h.
I'm here to pack some stuff.
Baseball said I could.
...
U-u-h-h.
Could I talk to some'un?
...
Will somebody talk to me?
KIPPY. *(To us.)* And almost nobody would. *(Lights. Kippy, Jason,
Martinez, Rodriguez, Kawabata dressing after the shower.)* And the
bad feeling continued — and took on an international flavor.
(Martinez and Rodriguez eye Kawabata with suspicion.)
MARTINEZ. *Mira lo primito, por ese es qué perdémos.*
RODRIGUEZ. *Por el es por qué siempre perdemos.*
MARTINEZ. *Hasta los juegos que el no lanza —*
RODRIGUEZ. *Sabemos que el —*
MARTINEZ. *Sabemos que nos va ha decojonar —*
RODRIGUEZ. *Sabemos que nos va ha cagar —*
JASON. *(Over last of this.)* Hey Kippy, do you know what they're
saying?
KIPPY. Kawabata sucks.
JASON. Oh.
MARTINEZ. *¿Siete millones — tu te ganas siete millones?*
JASON. Do you speak Spanish?
RODRIGUEZ. *Yo tengo suerte si me gano seis —*
KIPPY. I don't speak Spanish, but I understand it —
MARTINEZ. *Yo tengo suerte si me gano seis-punto-cinco —*
KIPPY. *"No hablo Espanol pero comprendolo"* —
RODRIGUEZ. *¡Oye, Nip, mama esto!*
MARTINEZ. *¡Mama* esto!
RODRIGUEZ. *¡No — mama esto!*
MARTINEZ. *¡No. Mama* esto!
RODRIGUEZ. *Oye muchacho, deja eso', el va a mamar* esto.
MARTINEZ. *El mio es mas lindo.*
RODRIGUEZ. *El mio es mas grande.*
MARTINEZ. Size queen!
RODRIGUEZ. *Maricon!*
MARTINEZ. *¿A quién tu le dices maricon? (They start to shove each*

other. Fight.)

JASON. What are they talking about now?

KIPPY. Dick.

JASON. Oh. *(Kawabata makes a guttural noise. Martinez and Rodriguez stop fighting. Kawabata stares at them, makes another guttural noise. Screams something.)* What's *he* saying?

KIPPY. He's asking if they've ever seen Akira Kurasowa's timeless masterpiece, *Throne of Blood? (Kawabata screams at them again. They go off.)*

JASON. What are they — ?

KIPPY. They didn't care for it.

JASON. You speak Japanese, too?

KIPPY. I don't speak Japanese but I understand it. Nogo pogo togo gogo: I don't speak Japanese but I understand it.

JASON. Howzat go?

KIPPY. Nogo pogo togo gogo.

JASON. Nogo gogo —

KIPPY. Nogo *pogo* —

JASON. Nogo *pogo*…?

KIPPY. Togo —

JASON. *Togo*…? *(Looks to Kippy for help. Kippy gestures with his hands "come on" like signaling a car to keep backing up. Jason looks helpless. Kippy dances a quick frug.)* Gogo!

KIPPY. You got it! *(Jason goes to Kawabata.)*

JASON. Nogo … pogo … togo … gogo. *(Kawabata gives him a funny look.)* Why's he looking at me like that?

KIPPY. Because, in truth, you neither speak nor understand Japanese. He senses this.

JASON. Uh-oh.

KAWABATA. *Kodoku na mondaze. Make tsuzukeru nowa. Hanashi aite nante ineh shi, kazoku mo tohku hanarete iru. Wakarukai, Kippy-san yo? Auta dake wa wakatte kureru yohna ki ga surunda.*

JASON. What's he —

KIPPY. He's saying he's lonely.

KAWABATA. *America …*

KIPPY. He's lonely here in America.

KAWABATA. *Ore no sobo mo mukashi koko ni sundeta. Sensoh ga hajimaruto kyohsei shuyohjo ni irerareta. Zaisan wa bosshu.*

KIPPY. His grandmother lived in this country — when the war came, she was interned — she was put in a camp —

JASON. Whazzat?

36

KIPPY. Read a book.

JASON. Nope.

KAWABATA. *Hiroshima to Nagasaki nimo ohkuno shinseki ga ita.*

KIPPY. He had relatives bombed to bits in both Hiroshima and Nagasaki — *(Anticipating Jason.)* Japanese cities we bombed in World War Two —

KAWABATA. *Ore no ie wa yurusu koto o shiranai mechakucha na senzo ni toritsukareta te ita.*

KIPPY. He says, he grew up in a house full of wrecked ancestors who never forgave anything.

KAWABATA. *Dairigu de nageru tameni America e kita toki, oremo yurusarenu mono no hitotsu ni natchimatta.*

KIPPY. When he came here to play in the major leagues, he became another thing not to forgive —

KAWABATA. *Yakyu o metafah dato yu hito mo iruga —*

KIPPY. He says, for many baseball is a metaphor —

KAWABATA. *Ore niwa yakyu igai ni nanimo nehndayo.*

KIPPY. But for him it's all, it's everything —

KAWABATA. *Katsu kotoga inochi de ari, makeru koto wa shinu yohna monda.*

KIPPY. When he wins, he lives; when he loses, he dies.

KAWABATA. *Sutoraiku Wan, Sutoraiku Tsuu, Sanshin.*

KIPPY. Strike One, Strike Two, Strike Three.

KAWABATA. *Kyoh, ore wa maketa. Kyoh, ore wa shinda nosa.*

KIPPY. "Tonight I lost. Tonight I am a dead man." *(Pause. Jason sobs.)*

JASON. This fucking — this *country,* man — it tears me up. *(He claps his hand onto Kawabata's shoulder.)* I know this isn't much, man, but — I feel your pain — and I apologize for my white people. *(Hugs him.)*

KAWABATA. *(Shakes him off.)* Faggot.

KIPPY. He says, thank you very much. *(Jason exits. Lights. Shane, solo.)*

SHANE. I'm just a dumb kid …

KIPPY. *(To us.)* You know about this part: The Letter. The famous letter that changed everything — you've read it in your paper, seen it read on television — these are just excerpts.

SHANE. I didn't know most'a'those words meant bad stuff, I just been hearin' them all my life.
The onliest thing I can do is throw — onliest thing I ever could do. I didn't mean to hurt anybody an' I accept full responsibility for my

speakings.

I should be punished.

KIPPY. There was something sort of heartrending about it. The spelling was so horrible — it was *authentic* somehow —

SHANE. Only please — I'm beggin' —

KIPPY. And then of course the story of his past started leaking out —

SHANE. Lemme back sometime —

KIPPY. That orphan business — the murder-suicide "attempt" —

SHANE. 'Cause I don't got any other place t'go.

KIPPY. And sympathy shifted … just a bit.

SHANE. Thank you. *(Out on Shane.)*

KIPPY. Here was one of life's castoffs. One of the people nobody ever took care of.

And it's possible that our love of punishment is exceeded only by our passion to forgive.

And what were a few words?

Especially when the words didn't match up with what was in his … would you call it *mind?*

Heart.

And baseball, which is flexible, started to reconsider. And nearly everybody was almost okay with that. *(Lights. Skipper's office. Skipper is seated. Darren enters.)*

DARREN. Uh, Skip, is it all right if we talk a minute?

SKIPPER. Oh sure, Darren, come on in.

DARREN. Thanks.

SKIPPER. This was another brutal loss, but you played well. I appreciate that, Darren. I appreciate that you can still function while the other guys are all stinkin' up the place.

DARREN. That's what I'm paid to do.

SKIPPER. And *hand*somely.

DARREN. … Yeah.

SKIPPER. What's on your mind?

DARREN. There's this rumor goin' 'round?

SKIPPER. Pay no attention to that.

DARREN. Then it's not true?

SKIPPER. I didn't say that. Frankly, I don't know what rumor you're talking about, there are so many. Don't pay attention to any of them.

DARREN. About Mungitt comin' back.

SKIPPER. Pay no attention to that.

DARREN. Now ya see, Skip, I don't know if you're tellin' me that because it's not *true* or if you're just enunciatin' a general *prin*ciple —

SKIPPER. Either way, same thing.

DARREN. Well no, it's not … sir.

Because if he's comin' back, I have to say I'd have a real problem with that.

SKIPPER. … You know I have no say in this decision, Darren. That's up to the Commissioner.

DARREN. But even if the Commissioner says it's okay, the Empires don't have to take him back — they can release him or send him down —

SKIPPER. *That's* up to the owner.

DARREN. Yeah, Skip, but all due respect, the guy I've got to talk to is *you.*

Now I think I'm a pretty important member of this team and —

SKIPPER. You're vital —

DARREN. — and I think my feelings should be listened to.

SKIPPER. *I'm* listening.

DARREN. Okay. So —

SKIPPER. 'Course I can't *do* squat about this situation —

DARREN. … Then he *is* comin' back?

SKIPPER. I don't know that. I mean, I can't say.

DARREN. The thing is, he can't. It'd disrupt the team morale.

SKIPPER. There's something you know about.

DARREN. … Pardon?

SKIPPER. No. Go on.

DARREN. Ya can't expect guys to be *able* to play with a guy that said stuff like that about 'em. Every day, it'd just be there. That's not right — that's bad for the team —

SKIPPER. A lotta things aren't "right," Darren —

DARREN. I know that Skip.

SKIPPER. All sorts of things aren't right —

DARREN. I know —

SKIPPER. Is it right, for instance, for somebody to land one of the fattest contracts in baseball history and *only then* reveal his interesting little personal quirk? Is *that* "right"? I ask you. *(Beat.)*

DARREN. Those things didn't have anything to do with each other.

SKIPPER. I didn't say they did. I'm just asking. *(Beat.)*

DARREN. *(Quiet.)* Oh. *(Beat.)* What he — they were — the things he said … they weren't in the spirit of a team. Guys, all sortsa' guys, they're really of*fended* and they shouldn't have to put up with that in their workplace. I'm not speaking about me. It's guys like Martinez and, uh …

SKIPPER. Rodriguez —

DARREN. *(Slighty overlap.)* Rodriguez. Kawabata.

SKIPPER. I've spoken to those guys. I spoke to them right after Mungitt's interview, in fact. I spoke to alla the guys. They're fine. They just want to play baseball. They just want to be part of this organization. They're willing to do what it takes, if it comes to that. You don't have to worry about them being offended. *(Pause.)*

DARREN. … *I'm* offended. Isn't that *enough?*

(Quietly.) I don't ask for things …

(Defiant.) I don't ask for things!

I'm *offended.* Isn't that enough? *(Beat. No response.)*

I'm speaking as an African-American, of course. *(Beat.)*

Not as a cocksucker.

SKIPPER. Aw shit, Darren — don't use — I don't think of you that way.

DARREN. You don't *visualize* me that way.

SKIPPER. Cut this crap. I have loved you like a son, Darren.

DARREN. … What tense was that? *(Beat.)*

SKIPPER. What happens, happens. It's out of my hands. You're very important to us. I hope you can adjust. You've always been able to adjust. Even to situations that *weren't* of your own making. You're a great player. Nobody doesn't appreciate that. Truly, Darren: *Nobody doesn't. (Skipper exits. Darren alone. Lights. Mason, solo.)*

MASON. So one night at about ten o'clock, I got a call. *(Darren appears.)*

DARREN. Mason, it's Darren, pick up.

MASON. *(To us.)* I screen. I picked up. Darren?

DARREN. I gotta talk to you.

MASON. Of course, of course. *(To us.)* But here was the situation: Right outside my apartment, my two homosexual neighbors from down the hall, who always look at me as if I'm wearing white shoes, were waiting for the elevator. They were walking their horrible exotic little dog — a shiatsu, a jujitsu, I don't know — it's not even a dog, really, it's a dogette. Now two months earlier, Darren Lemming would have meant nothing to them, but now their conversation was *infested* with, oh, the infield *fly* rule and "they need more pop in their lineup" — so I said: *(Loudly:)* Darren? Is that you?

DARREN. Yeah.

MASON. Why, Mr. Lemming, what a pleasant surprise! *(To us:)* And Darren said:

DARREN. Are those two gay guys in the hall again?

MASON. … No.

DARREN. Yeah, they are.

MASON. Um —

DARREN. Quit it, all right. I'm in a bad mood.

MASON. I'm sorry …

DARREN. No I am.

Listen, stop with the talking loud, one day I'll come to your place, we'll ride in the elevator with those guys, I'll kiss you on the mouth; deal?

MASON. Ha.

DARREN. Listen, Mars, I need to see you. Soon.

MASON. *(To us.)* Mars?

DARREN. There's some serious stuff I gotta talk to you about. Would'j'a meet me after the game tomorrow?

MASON. Oh — okay. Where?

DARREN. Why don't'ch'a finally come to a game? I'll give 'em your name. You can meet me in the clubhouse after.

MASON. Oh no. I don't think so.

DARREN. Why not?

MASON. Not the clubhouse. I'd be … overwhelmed.

DARREN. Just hang out then. I'll meet you where you're sitting.

MASON. Where *will* I be —

DARREN. Don't worry. There'll be waiter service, Mars.

MASON. Mars?

DARREN. Ya need a nickname.

MASON. … I'm not worthy.

DARREN. You're worthy.

MASON. What's *yours?*

DARREN. No. I *don't* need a nickname. *(Out on Darren.)*

MASON. And the next night, I was at the game.

And maybe I've had a ridiculous life, but this was one of its best nights. *(And we see: baseball. Some sort of stylized but not too dancey evocation of it.)* The seats, as promised, were excellent. The game, at first, profoundly demoralizing.

By the third inning, we were trailing seven-nothing.

The crowd was vocal. Because the subject here was *baseball* and the stadium was full of scholars — historians — and soon enough I found myself engaged in learned debate with all these … strangers, these … *guys.*

As for the last several weeks I'd been conversing with all *sorts* of

41

people I'd never been able to speak to before: *Cab*drivers.

My five brothers.

Then, with two outs in the bottom of the ninth, the miracle happened. *(And may we see some version of this?)*

We got a hit.

Then another.

Then another.

And another and another and —

Think: Mets versus Braves June thirtieth, 2000 — where the Mets went into the eighth losing eight to one and scored *ten runs* in a *single* inning to take the game eleven-eight.

And we took *this* game.

And when the winning run crossed home plate, the fans who had stayed rose in this single surge and let out a shout like the "Hallelujah Chorus."

And it was the first crowd I had ever agreed with.

… Security had been alerted that I'd be waiting so they let me be. And for several minutes, I had an entire stadium entirely to myself. And that was thrilling. *(Darren enters.)* You nodded to me.

DARREN. Whazzat?

MASON. I saw you do it.

DARREN. Yeah, well, I *know* you.

MASON. But … you nodded.

DARREN. What's the big deal?

MASON. It *is* … it is a big deal.

What a game!

What an amazing thing!

Thank you for it.

DARREN. Yeah … well … whatever.

Listen, there's some stuff I wanna ask you about —

MASON. And that ninth inning!

DARREN. Yeah, it was good —

MASON. It was *more* than "good." It was … *moving*, it was —

DARREN. Right, right —

MASON. A *lesson* — it *taught* me something —

DARREN. You're not gonna start in*terp*reting again, are ya?

MASON. I know, I know, I say to myself: The bat's of wood, the players number nine, the ball was manufactured in Costa Rica and that's all there is to it.

But I can't stop there. Baseball is … unre*lent*ingly *mean*ingful.

Tonight — eight runs in the ninth inning to win what looked like

42

a shutout; it taught me that —
DARREN. — it's never too late.
MASON. Yes!
And in my life it's never been early so you can imagine …
DARREN. … Yeah, okay —
MASON. Yes — oh um — so: this "stuff" you want to talk to me about?
DARREN. How'm I fixed for retirement? *(Beat.)*
MASON. You're a very wealthy man.
DARREN. Wealthy for life? *(Beat.)*
MASON. Certainly.
And with the ten or fifteen years of baseball that are surely left in you, there's no telling —
DARREN. What if I retired sooner?
MASON. I'm sure that …
How much sooner? *(Beat.)*
DARREN. Tomorrow morning. *(Beat. Mason laughs as if it were a joke. Darren isn't laughing. Mason stops laughing.)*
MASON. … No …
DARREN. So I'd run out of money. *(Beat.)*
MASON. Yes.
DARREN. Bullshit.
MASON. I'm —
What are you…?
What *is* this? Some sort of game you're torturing me with?
DARREN. I'm thinkin' of makin' an announcement.
MASON. … Well, that's preposterous.
Well, that just can't *be*.
DARREN. I just want you to assure me that —
MASON. Well, I won't, I refuse to.
DARREN. Well, fuck you, then. *(Beat.)*
MASON. You can't retire — to*mor*row.
DARREN. I think I might.
MASON. You're playing against Davey Battle tomorrow. That's your favorite thing to do. You said so in *S.I.* — May 12th, 19—
DARREN. Well, I haven't spoken to him in a while —
MASON. But it's your favorite —
DARREN. Maybe not anymore. *(Beat.)*
MASON. This is all about that piece of white trash coming back tomorrow, isn't it?
DARREN. Nah, it's —

MASON. They're bringing him back without even consulting you and that's a blow to your pride. He insulted you and humiliated you and you've never experienced that because four people a century are *spared*. Of course that all makes this an agonizing time for you —

DARREN. No, Mars — uh-uh. It's been sorta a *flat* time.

MASON. … Don't say *that* —

DARREN. I'm just sorta tired of it.

MASON. You can't do this. It's too important —

DARREN. Fuck the gay community —

MASON. I *would* but they don't *want* to but that's not the *point*. That's not what I'm talking about.

DARREN. Then what *are* you talkin' about? *(Beat.)* You? *(Pause.)*

MASON. Yes. *(Pause.)* I have been watching baseball nonstop since the day I was told you were coming to me.

And at first it was a chore. I understood nothing.

I couldn't tell one player from another.

And then I *could*.

And it wasn't a chore any longer, it was … this … astonishment! This … *abundance*.

So much to learn, so much to memorize.

… When you're not playing now, I watch whoever is; when there's no one playing, I watch tapes from twenty years ago, when I'm out of tapes, I read books.

I've been *crying* for two months.

That's a ridiculous, that's a disgusting thing to say.

I hate people who tell you how they're *crying*. "Oh, I'm so deep — it's so meaningful — I *cried*."

Bullshit.

I'm telling you *because* it's ludicrous — I *know* it's ludicrous.

But Darren, I *never* cry about *any*thing. I only ever have about *two* feelings a year; and all of a sudden … *(He spreads his arms, speechless.)* I'm having *memories*.

Playing catch with Dad. Going to games over summer vacation. They're not even *my memories* but I'm *hav*ing them.

I don't get it. I don't get any of it.

I don't know why I feel exalted when we win.

I don't know why I feel diminished when we lose.

I don't know why I'm saying "we"…!

Life is so … tiny, so *dai*ly. This … you … take me out of it …

I know … things are hard for you now … I know it's a difficult time … but don't tell me you're *flat*. Be in agony, but don't be indifferent. Look where we are! Smell the air!

DARREN. This is kinda sentimental.

MASON. I *want* to be sentimental! I want to be … *(He makes a gesture with his whole body. It's clunky but weirdly graceful. Darren laughs. Mason realizes it's not a mocking laugh and laughs himself. Pause.)* Promise me you won't retire.

DARREN. Mars —

MASON. Promise me you won't retire tomorrow morning.

DARREN. … Mars —

MASON. For *me*. I'm your *business* manager. *(Beat.)*

DARREN. I won't retire tomorrow morning.

MASON. … Thank you, Darren.

DARREN. Day after, maybe.

MASON. *(To us.)* Which would already have been too late. *(Lights. Kippy, solo.)*

KIPPY. Then the day came and we were playing Davey Battle and his lousy team.

And Shane Mungitt was making his long-derided return. And who knew those two facts would mean anything to each other? This was the first time Darren and Davey had spoken since the "thing." Davey came into our clubhouse — which is totally illegal even for superstars. He took Darren aside and they talked.

And I saw Davey on the way out. *(Davey enters.)*

Hey … Davey …

DAVEY. Mr. Sunderstrom, how are you, my man? *(Elaborate hand-shake thing.)*

KIPPY. I'm not bad, not bad, my man.

DAVEY. And your wife, and your three, my man?

KIPPY. Who ever sees them? Okay, I guess, my man.

And how's Linda?

DAVEY. Excellent, excellent …

KIPPY. And Ta-whosis and Ta-whatsis and little Davey Junior?

DAVEY. Profoundly well, thank you. *(Beat.)*

KIPPY. So, what are you doing in our clubhouse, Davey? That violates a really sacred rule.

DAVEY. Well, *some* violations are necessary, aren't they, my man?

KIPPY. Okay, sure. *(Beat.)* So you and Darren … talked?

DAVEY. Oh, yes.

KIPPY. And that went…?

DAVEY. … It certainly did.

KIPPY. … well?

DAVEY. Of course it went well. All things go well when two people speak their truth.

KIPPY. *(To us.)* I know I'm not supposed to say this, but he was a very bombastic guy …

DAVEY. You're very … *fond* of Darren, aren't you?

KIPPY. Umm … .yes? I'm not sure in what sense you mean the word but yes. Immensely fond. *(Hesitation.)*

DAVEY. I wish you a good game, my man.

KIPPY. You as well, my man.

DAVEY. We're gonna whup your ass.

KIPPY. We're gonna kill you. *(Lights. To us.)* Did I tell you about Shane Mungitt's cleanliness thing?

Shane Mungitt had a cleanliness thing.

He had a ritual of three showers before the game,

two showers after.

In the Emp clubhouse, the showers are located off the main room and down a fairly lengthy hallway.

So I didn't know — and wouldn't learn for months — that, as I was talking with Davey Battle, Shane was performing his third pre-game ritual shower — *(Lights on Shane, showering.)* And he wasn't alone. *(Fade on Kippy. Darren enters shower, hangs up towel. Shane, at first, is not aware of him.)*

DARREN. … Hey! *(Shane looks at him.)*

SHANE. … Hey …

DARREN. Welcome. Welcome back. *(Beat.)*

SHANE. U-u-u-u-h-h …

DARREN. You've been missed.

SHANE. … Thanks. *(Turns away, keeps showering.)*

DARREN. So you take a lotta showers … don't'ch'a?

SHANE. … Yeah.

DARREN. An' now I'm here beside you. Ya know what *that* means, don't'cha? *(Shane looks at him.)* Cleanliness is next to godliness, HA!

SHANE. … Why'n't ya leave me alone?

DARREN. So, I'm wonderin', Shane? These ablutions…?

SHANE. … I don't know that word …

DARREN. All these showers ya take. You just tryin' to scrub away the skin? You tryin' to get through all these layers'f tissue an' organs 'n'stuff to get to where the real dirt lies?

SHANE. … You wunt who I meant.

DARREN. Whazzat?

SHANE. You wunt who I's talkin' about.
You wunt the faggot.

DARREN. Oh no?
Who was?

SHANE. … Some other coupla guys …

DARREN. *Name* them. *(Beat.)*

SHANE. Why'n't ya leave me alone?

DARREN. Aw, Shane, listen … you're not gettin' me. I *know.*

SHANE. … Huh?

DARREN. I understand.
An' it's okay.

SHANE. … Huh?

DARREN. People … when they lash out like that … for no reason like that … they're lashin' out at what they fear.
At what they fear they *are.*

SHANE. … Huh?

DARREN. You're colored, aren't ya, Shane?

SHANE. … U-u-h-h … *No.*

DARREN. You're a colored guy.

SHANE. Nah. *(Beat.)*

DARREN. Aw, I was just goofin' on ya.

SHANE. Why'n't ya leave me alone?

DARREN. You're not colored.

SHANE. U-u-u-h-h … *(Shane turns around, back to Darren. Darren rushes him, embraces him from behind.)*

DARREN. It's right — I know it.

SHANE. HEY! HEY! HEY!

DARREN. I feel it, too.
I have since the beginning …

SHANE. HEY! HEY! HEY!

DARREN. We don't have to tell the others —

SHANE. HEY! HEY! HEY! *(Shane's fighting him off, Darren kisses him. Shane thrashes his way out of Darren's embrace.)* FUCKER!
U-u-h-h …
FUCKER!
U-u-h-h …
FUCKER!

DARREN. Our little secret. *(Shane is mortified.)* You dumb cracker fuck. *(Lights. Kippy, solo.)*

KIPPY. So then we had a ball game.

And it was bizarre right from the beginning.

Bottom of the first, no score.

The first three Empires hit home runs.

The next three strike out and we don't score again for the whole game.

Which, strangely, is okay.

Because Kawabata is perfect through eight.

Which meant that, in the *bottom* of the eighth, conditions in the dugout were excruciating. *(In the dugout: Rodriguez and Martinez sit together, eating and spitting out sunflower seeds. Jason is near them. Skipper stands. Kawabata sits away from everybody. Toddy paces.)*

TODDY. Don't talk to the fucker, don't talk to the fucker, fucker's got a perfect game going, don't talk to the fucker. Do ya hear me? Don't talk to the fucker, don't talk to the fucker, whatever you do, don't *talk* to the —

SKIPPER. Toddy!

TODDY. Yeah, Skip?

SKIPPER. Nobody ever talks to the fucker, the fucker doesn't speak English.

KIPPY. Finally, it's the top of the ninth. *(Kawabata up and pitching.)* And like *that* there are two outs.

Kawabata is one out away from a perfect game.

One out away from no bullpen, no collapse —

No Shane Mungitt.

Kawabata set up. *(He does.)* He delivered. *(He does.)* And — ! *(SFX: The hitter getting all of it.)* Home Run. *(Kawabata watches it leave the park.)* Which was followed by a single which was followed by a triple. And suddenly we're ahead by only one run with the go-ahead run at the plate. *(Skipper goes to mound, collects ball, pats Kawabata on the back. Kawabata leaves, tips hat to crowd.)* To a roar of approval and frustration and gratitude and sorrow, Kawabata left the game. And for the first time since his suspension, Shane came in. *(Shane enters.)* And the crowd cheered him, too — whatever *that* meant.

And Shane seemed intense on the mound — even for him.

He had this internal monologue going; it was so fierce,

it seemed like you could hear what he was thinking.

SHANE. Fuck fuck fuck fuck fuck fuck fuck fuck fuck fuck fuck fuck fuck …

KIPPY. And I looked over to Darren who'd been really quiet and solitary the whole game. And he looked like he could murder somebody. *(Focus on Darren, scarily still.)* And Shane faced his first batter.

Who was Davey Battle.

And Darren had that weird look I'd never seen before. *(Davey Battle is poised to swing.)* And Shane looked strange even for *him.* And he threw his first pitch. *(Shane throws.)* And it hit Davey. And Davey went down. *(Davey crumples.)* And he never got up.

End of Act Two

ACT THREE

Kawabata, solo.

KAWABATA. This is a very hard, a very lonely time.
All day long, wherever you go, on every screen, you see it replayed:
A single act.
At several speeds, from various angles.
Slow-motion. Catcher-cam.
"Massive Trauma to the Head."
Too much — one must look away.
In the clubhouse, there is steady noise, a constant low hum of conversation.
But I am very fortunate;
My first act in the major leagues was to dismiss my translator.
It's served me well.
I know all the English necessary to me:
Sutoraiku Wan. Sutoraiku Tsuu. Sanshin.
Shall I be saying to myself:
"If only that pitch had been less fat, if only I had gotten that third out"?
No.
Why must things have meanings?
This is how I try to be an American: I make my mind a prairie.
I think nothing. I think of great flat stretches of nothing. *(Kawabata winds up, delivers.)* It soothes me. *(Lights. Darren paces. A phone rings. Lights on Mason.)*
MASON. Hello?
DARREN. It's me —
MASON. — Oh! —
DARREN. It's Darren —
MASON. I — yes I *know* — *(Loudly:)* Well, what do you know? Darren Lemming! Why are you calling —
DARREN. Are the gay guys just gettin' back from a club or somethin'?
MASON. ... Um. Yes.

50

DARREN. Oh. I figured …

MASON. … It was today, wasn't it?

DARREN. Yeah, uh-huh.

MASON. … I'm very sorry, Darren.

DARREN. There were all these ballplayers in these beautiful black suits. The guys from *his* team sat way up close an' later they were pallbearers, some'a'them. An' our guys were sorta hushed an' way back an' it was like we were gonna have a truce 'cause it was a sacred thing this thing that was goin' on. *(Beat.)* An' this one time I locked eyes with Linda, with Davey's wife, an' it was like she was trying to tell me something. If only you hadn'a' done this … if only you hadn'a' done that … *(Beat.)* I keep thinkin'. If only I hadn'a' done this or that … If only I hadn'a' done this *an'* that … *(Beat.)* You were up, right?

MASON. Yes.

DARREN. I figured you were up. I don't know many people who're up this time'a'night. *(Beat.)* I don't know many people.

MASON. Neither do I.

DARREN. I don't really have friends.

MASON. That's not true.

DARREN. No, it is.

Somethin' I realized the other day.

I've sorta … I haven't been on a level enough playing field, ya know? *(Pause.)*

MASON. Darren?

DARREN. IT'S HIS OWN FUCKIN' FAULT. IF HE HADN'A…! *(He calms down.)* So what's up with *you?*

MASON. Well …

DARREN. Somebody talk to me about *you* for a change …

MASON. Wellll … I — *(There's a beep tone.)*

DARREN. Wait a second, I got another call … Yeah? *(Lights on Kippy.)*

KIPPY. It's Kippy.

DARREN. Hey.

KIPPY. I'm not waking you, am I?

DARREN. 'Course not.

KIPPY. What a fuck of a day, huh?

DARREN. Yeah.

KIPPY. My kids are all messed up. All day I'm telling them: The ball is *good;* the ball is not *evil.* Daddy plays a *game;* Daddy is not at *war.* I wish I drank.

DARREN. I wish *I* drank. *(Beat.)*

KIPPY. Darren ... I'm sorry I didn't like Davey enough.

DARREN. He had some stuff —

KIPPY. I don't think it was about him, I think it was about *you.* He was always your best friend, you know, and I was just your best friend on the *team.* Mine had an asterisk. I think I was probably jealous —

DARREN. That's okay, Kippy.

KIPPY. Darren ... You know I love you, right?

...

...

I know that's *fraught* given the circumstances, but you know I mean it in the un-fraught sort of way, don't you?

DARREN. Yeah, sure, Kippy, I get it.

I don't know why you wanna *bring* it up, right now.

KIPPY. I want to *say* something.

...

People have to talk.

DARREN. Do they? *(Pause.)*

KIPPY. I think they do.

I still think they do.

Good night, Darren. *(He hangs up. Pause. Darren clicks off.)*

DARREN. Shit.

MASON. Hello?

DARREN. Oh, Mason! I forgot about ya.

MASON. I invented a wonderful new pasta dish!

DARREN. ... So?

MASON. You wanted ... to talk about me.

DARREN. Oh!

Oh right.

Well ... maybe I don't.

MASON. ... Are they going to arrest him?

DARREN. What?

MASON. Shane?

DARREN. *What — ?*

MASON. Shane Mungitt.

They say there's reason to believe — I *heard* — he made vague ... threats.

DARREN. ... When ... did —

MASON. Before the game — he was coming out of the shower and some guys overheard him —

52

DARREN. *(Overlaps.)* He was comin' out of the —

MASON. Yeah — did you not hear this? *(Toddy, Jason, Martinez, Rodriguez and Kawabata appear in suits.)* After the funeral some of the guys felt moved or guilty or something and they spoke to the press.

TODDY. It's not like ya ever listened to Shane Mungitt.

JASON. Mostly we tried not to listen to Shane Mungitt.

TODDY. But he was pretty stressed comin' outta the shower —

JASON. Even for *him* —

TODDY. The thing is, we thought that was encouraging 'cause he's one'a' those guys who when he's angry —

JASON. It's *good* when he's angry —

TODDY. He can spot when he's angry —

JASON. When he isn't angry, he can't locate his pitches so good?

TODDY. But, so, anyway, he *passed* us comin' out of the shower an' he said —

JASON. "I *hate* you all" —

TODDY. To all of us —

JASON. To everybody —

TODDY. He just said —

JASON. "I *hate* you all."

TODDY. … Anyway, we thought that was encouraging —

JASON. We thought, okay, today he's gonna have control —

MARTINEZ. *Pendejo* —

RODRIGUEZ. *Pendejo* —

JASON. But then he said —

TODDY. He said —

JASON. "You watch me when I get out there — I'm gonna *kill* somebody — I'm gonna take somebody out."

TODDY. … Anyway, we thought that was encouraging.

JASON. Yeah, we did. *(They disappear.)*

MASON. And at the time they thought it was just sportsmanlike but … after … it seemed …

It was on CNN …

Darren?

DARREN. They *should* arrest him.

…

They should arrest everybody.

MASON. Darren?

DARREN. They should arrest *me. (Lights.)*

KIPPY. Darren's last encounter with Davey Battle. *(Lights. Darren and Davey.)*

53

DARREN. I ... uh ... we haven't talked ...

DAVEY. No, Darren, we haven't ...

DARREN. ... You get my messages, Davey?

DAVEY. Now that's very interesting, Darren.
That's a very interesting way to *put it.*
"Did I get your messages?"
Not your "message" not singular — no, you ask:
Did I get your messages?
And I can only answer: some of them.
Some I *failed* to get.
Some, it seems, were never *sent.*

DARREN. Shit, Davey, it was just a *ques*tion —

DAVEY. Don't touch me!

DARREN. I'm ten feet away from ya, Davey —

DAVEY. And we should keep that distance. We should maintain
that distance from which things can be seen in their *entirety.*

DARREN. ... Okay.

DAVEY. This is a day of *reck*oning. *(Darren makes a lightly scoffing
sound.)* Are you *fleering* at me, Darren?

DARREN. I wouldn't know it if I was.
Fleering!
Why do you talk like you were born a hundred years ago?

DAVEY. And what if I do?

DARREN. I dunno.
It's just a little uncontemporary.

DAVEY. And is that a *bad* thing, Darren?
Do we *value* the present over all other epochs?
Do we think everything has evolved in the direction of the good? Or
has some of it — most of it — been a sliding back? A devolution?

DARREN. Aw, shit, you're not gonna start disclaimin' dinosaurs
on me and stuff, are ya?

DAVEY. I'm just saying, Darren, that it is more often than not a
small mind that considers itself en*light*ened. That en*light*enment is
most often an inability to see the darkness that surrounds you. *(Beat.)*

DARREN. This isn't gonna go well, is it?

DAVEY. Oh I think it is.
I think it is going to go well, Darren.
How can things go badly when two people speak their truth? *(Beat.)*

DARREN. Fleer.

DAVEY. *Are you making mock of me?*

DARREN. Only a little, Davey — the way you like —

DAVEY. That's over.

DARREN. ... Okay.

DAVEY. Who the *fuck* are you, man? What the *fuck* do you think you're doing here?

DARREN. I —

DAVEY. What kind of *mess* do you find it fit to make? What kind of *nonsense* are you putting out in the world?

DARREN. I —

DAVEY. "*I!*" "*I!*" — Stop saying "I" — you don't know the meaning of the word —

DARREN. But I do, Davey —

DAVEY. *Shit*, man, we all have *demons*. Some of us less disgusting ones than yours — but we shut up about them! Take them into little rooms, *wrestle* with them there — present a good face to the world — till our demons are slain and we *become* what we claim we *are*.

What kind of sordidness is this you've got going on? Why did you feel the *need* to splash your ugliness all over everything.

DARREN. You told me to.

DAVEY. ... Oh, so now you feel some need to add *slander* to the mischief?

DARREN. I thought you were givin' me a sorta per*mis*sion, Davey, I thought you were bein' ... *kind*.

DAVEY. You twist everything.

DARREN. You told me to reveal my true nature.

You said I could only do this through love.

DAVEY. That's before I knew you were a pervert. *(Beat.)*

DARREN. Oh. *(Beat.)* You said you knew me to be good.

I ... loved you very much for that, Davey —

DAVEY. Have you just been wanting to *fuck* me for eight years, Darren?

DAVEY. No.

DAVEY. Have I been your *beard?*

DARREN. My...?

DAVEY. Oh, everybody knows Davey Battle's good, Davey Battle's a religious man, a continent man — nobody going around with Davey Battle's going to be whoring, nobody going around with Davey Battle's going to be chasing tail — was that the whole thing, Darren?

DARREN. I don't — think so —

DAVEY. Then *what?*

DARREN. I liked you. *(Beat.)*

DAVEY. You lie.

DARREN. Fuck you —

DAVEY. You lie in your heart —

DARREN. Fuck you, Davey, fuck you —

DAVEY. And until you correct yourself —

DARREN. *Fuck* yourself, man — *fuck* yourself —

DAVEY. You will welter in profanity and vulgarity and every kind of ugliness.

DARREN. You're right.

Yes, you're right.

I need to clean up my language.

I need to make my language family-appropriate

while at the same time conveyin' the *truth* of my heart so let me just put it *this* way, Davey:

Drop dead. *(Lights. Lights on: Darren, solo.)* And then I took a shower and then we played a game. *(Light shift.)*

KIPPY. So now we start the Kafkaesque portion of the evening.

Well, Kafka-lite, anyway ... Dekaf-ka.

After Shane killed Davey with the pitch, the question arose: Under whose jurisdiction does this event fall?

Major League Baseball immediately suspended him from the game. And we know how final *that* is.

But with this other evidence, there was some sense that this was not wildness, this was *murder*.

Shane was detained for questioning. *(Shane appears.)*

And he said ... nothing.

He just sort of alternated silence and babble.

At last, more out of frustration than anything, and probably rhetorically, they asked:

Is there *anyone* you'll talk to?

Will you talk to *anyone*, Shane?

And he said:

SHANE. Kippy.

KIPPY. He said:

SHANE. I wanna talk to Kippy.

KIPPY. I didn't have to go, it was made clear to me. And there were so many reasons not to. I decided I wouldn't.

Then that I would.

Then that I wouldn't.

Then, suddenly, I had a weird revelation:

I *wanted* to go. *(Darren appears.)* And when Darren asked me:

DARREN. Why?

KIPPY. I could only tell him what up till then I had always believed:

People have to talk.

DARREN. Do you think that fuck's *gonna* talk?

Do you think he's gonna *tell* you things?

KIPPY. He might, I told him.

It's possible he will.

And then, amazingly, Darren announced:

DARREN. I'm comin' with you.

KIPPY. And he *did.*

Did we both somehow suspect what would be found out there?

And did we *want* it found out for some reason?

I still don't know. I can't say.

All I know is there was a room. And there was hardly anything in it. Except for Darren. And me.

And Shane. *(And the room has taken form: a table, some chairs; the three of them.)*

SHANE. What's *that* one doin' here?

KIPPY. Well, Shane, Darren came here with me because —

SHANE. I didn't ask ta see *that* one, Kippy, I asked ta see *you* —

DARREN. I —

SHANE. Whut you doin' bringin' —

KIPPY. We're here, Shane, because everybody feels terrible about everything that happened. And we want to talk about it and clear it all up ... so we can move on. *(Shane starts to protest.)* We're here because we want to *help* you, Shane. *(Beat. Shane looks back and forth between them, suspicious, grumbles something. Tentatively, he decides to accept it, sits. Kippy sits then; then Darren either does or doesn't. An awkwardness.)*

SHANE. Some pitch, huh?

KIPPY. Yes, it was. It certainly was ... some kind of pitch.

SHANE. Both'a'ya'?

KIPPY. ... Pardon?

SHANE. Wanna help me?

Both'aya do? *(Beat.)*

DARREN. *(Quiet.)* Yeah.

SHANE. 'Cause I'd like'ta be helped.

KIPPY. That's good, Shane.

SHANE. That's why I wannid ta talk ta ya in the first place —

KIPPY. I'm glad.

SHANE. 'Cause it's still not too late.

KIPPY. Well, that's what we're thinking too, Shane.

SHANE. I can still contribute —

KIPPY. You can ... take your place in society and —

SHANE. 'Cause there are still, like, forty games left an' 'f'I could get back in a *week,* I could —

KIPPY. Shane —

SHANE. — contribute — 'cause —

KIPPY. Shane?

You killed a guy. You threw a pitch and it *killed* a guy.

SHANE. ... Yeah, okay, that's *true.* On the other hand —

KIPPY. You threw a pitch; a man is *dead.*

SHANE. ... Okay, like, if you're gonna *harp* on that —

KIPPY. A *man* is *dead* because you *threw* a *ball. (Pause.)*

SHANE. Okay, so, even if it takes *three* weeks I could still contribute 'cause —

KIPPY. That won't happen.

SHANE. ... Why *not?*

KIPPY. Shane: You are no longer desired in baseball.

SHANE. ... Well

u-u-u-h-h

that's *wrong.*

That's just not — that's wrong.

I think I should be *more* desired.

I think — now — I can be more u-u-h-h

ef*fec*tive than ever.

KIPPY. No, Shane, you can't.

SHANE. Nobody's gonna be hoggin' the plate on me, now, Kippy. I *own* the plate.

Other guys — they gotta, they gotta *get* it

ev'y time they go out there — but not me, not now.

I can really per*form* now. I can *ex*ecute. *(Beat.)* Even if it's three-an'-a-*half* weeks —

KIPPY. It's not gonna be three-and-a-half weeks —

SHANE. Well, longer'n *that* an' it'll be meanin'less, so —

KIPPY. You are never going to pitch again, Shane. *(Beat. Shane looks at Kippy, blankly. Shane bursts into wracking sobs. They build, then subside.)* I'm sorry.

SHANE. Why'd ya haveta say shit like that for?

KIPPY. I'm —

SHANE. Ya think I'm not depressed enough already?

KIPPY. I'm —

SHANE. Fuck. Fuck.

KIPPY. … Forgive me. *(Beat.)*

SHANE. *(Points to Darren.)* WHY'S HE KEEP LOOKIN' AT ME LIKE THAT? *(To Darren.)* WHY'D'YA KEEP LOOKIN' AT ME LIKE THAT?

DARREN. *(Blandly.)* You're the scenery.

SHANE. THAT'S NOT *NICE!*

DARREN. You're outa your fuckin' —

KIPPY. Darren is not *not* being nice. Darren is a little outflanked by the situation. As we all are —

SHANE. I never did nothin' to him —

KIPPY. Well, *that* may be a case of selective memory but —

SHANE. He's a one who tried to do stuff to me — *(Beat.)* Fuckin' faggot. *(Darren lunges over the table; Kippy intervenes.)*

KIPPY. *Darren* — !

SHANE. Oh whut? You gonna *'tack* me again? You think that's helpful? *(Darren is stopped by this; moves away.)* You got a violen' nature, ya know that?

KIPPY. Darren does not have a —

SHANE. I'm jus' tryin' t'get a handle on things, ya know.

I keep bein' in these sitch'ations, I dunno.

U-u-h-h …

Th'own inta these sitch'ations.

With all these … colored people and whatnot —

DARREN. *Fuck* — !

KIPPY. Why do you *say* stuff like that, Shane?

SHANE. Whut?

DARREN. FUCK!

KIPPY. We are trying to *help* you — why do you have to say things like *colored* people —

SHANE. There's nothin' wrong with 'at — at's 'ceptable — They call themselves that —

KIPPY. They don't call themselves "colored people," they call themselves "people of color" —

SHANE. Whut's the difference? *(Beat.)*

KIPPY. We just have to take it on faith that there *is* one.

SHANE. I don't got any'a' *that,* Kippy. Faith. You know that.

KIPPY. Why did you throw that pitch, Shane? *(Shane laughs in that unhinged way.)* Shane.

SHANE. Well, 'at's a dumb *question,* Kippy. I'm a pitcher —

whut's I s'pose' t'do?

KIPPY. But why did you throw *that* pitch, Shane?

SHANE. ... I only *got* one pitch, Kippy. That's why I'm in short relief.

KIPPY. Were you trying to take him out? *(Beat. Shane nods.)*

SHANE. Of the *inning*.

That's my *job*.

Why'd I haveta sit here and get

u-u-u-h-h all

*ques*tions 'bout doin' my job?

That's not nice. *(Beat.)* Why ya askin' me this

u-u-h-h

crap? (Beat.) You my friend, Kippy?

KIPPY. ... Sure.

SHANE. 'Cause you were the only one'd ever *reach* out t'me. On the whole team. *That* one never did — 'cept t'try t'*rape* me one time — that's not nice —

DARREN. You *fuck* — I didn't try to —

SHANE. Ya ever have a half-breed faggot come at ya in a shower, huh, Kippy? It can —

KIPPY. What are you talking a — *(To Darren:)* What is he — ? *(And Darren shakes his head, trying to dismiss it, but also guilty, and turns away from Kippy. Kippy registers this, then, quickly, refuses it.)* Don't *say* that stuff, Shane —

SHANE. Why's ev'rybody so upset about?

I'm just tellin' the truth.

I'm just sayin whut's in my *heart* —

I'n'at whut I'm s'poseta do?

I'n'at whut you always say, Kippy —

KIPPY. That's *not* what's in your heart, Shane.

SHANE. ... No?

Oh.

I thought it was.

KIPPY. Why did you throw that —

SHANE. *WHY DO YA KEEP ASKIN' ME THE SAME THING ALLA TIME?* WHAT'S IT *TO* YA?

KIPPY. Shane!

A terrible thing has happened.

A terrible thing has happened precipitated by you.

The terrible thing that has happened and that was precipitated by you is of an indeterminate nature.

We are trying to *hone* in on you — on your thoughts — on the inner workings of your — on your motivations — in order to make the *in*determinate de*termi*nate.

That is our mission here, *Shane. (Beat.)*

DARREN. Well, I'm sure he got alla *that* one, Kippy.

SHANE. Why?

KIPPY. What?

SHANE. Why'd ya wanna make the inde ... de...?

KIPPY. Because known things are bearable in a way that unknown things are not. *(Beat.)*

SHANE. Oh. *(Beat.)* I dunno 'f' I agree.

Seems to me there's

u-u-u-h-h

lotsa stuff I would'a' rather not know.

Seems to me, I'd rather not know *most'a'* the stuff there *is.*

DARREN. That's 'cause you're a fuckin' moron —

SHANE. HEY! HEY! HEY! DON'T YOU CALL ME THOSE WORDS, THAT'S NOT NICE!

KIPPY. Shane, Darren doesn't *mean* what he says. Darren is just very upset because the man you *killed* — whether by accident or design — was his best friend — you can imagine that —

SHANE. *(Overlaps.)* Well, I dunno 'bout that —

KIPPY. *(Continuous.)* — that leads to rather strong — what?

SHANE. "Best friend." I dunno 'bout that.

KIPPY. Uh, that's not for you to decide

SHANE. I don't say shit like that to *my* best friend.

DARREN. Shit like *what?*

SHANE. All this "fuck you fuck you."

KIPPY. What are you talking about?

SHANE. All this "drop dead."

I wouldn'n' say that to *my* best friend — no sir — I would not —

KIPPY. You seem — not to have too firm a grip on —

SHANE. That's whut he said, that's whut he said, you just ask him!

DARREN. You sonuva —

SHANE. Right before he came into the shower and tried to rape me — I passed right by — right by him an' that dead guy — an' he was all "This this this this this" an' "that that that that that" an' "*Fuck* you *Fuck* you DROP DEAD!" Shit, why are ya askin' me what I wanted — he's the one who wisht it! He gave the order, I just executed — *(And Darren is too paralyzed to lash out.)* Shit, this

61

is no fun at *all!* You come here this *vis*it — ya don't even bring *food* — ask alla these questions. Fuck, what's all this about? One more dead colored guy — who the fuck cares?

KIPPY. Stop —

SHANE. That's what they're *for* — colored people — to get dead — that's what they're put on earth for, anyway —

KIPPY. *Stop.*

SHANE. Shit, they're not even people, niggers — they're only two-fifths of people — that's the *law* —

KIPPY. Just stop —

SHANE. That's the law *on* the books — ya know whut that makes *that* one? Half'a'him's two-fifths a person, the other half's all *fag*got he shouldn'n' even be walkin' upright —

KIPPY. SHUT UP!

SHANE. Oh, so now I'm s'pose'ta *shut up?* I thought I's s'pose'ta *speak up!*

DARREN. You fuck! Why did you throw that ball?

SHANE. WHUT WAS IN MY *HEART?*

IS *THAT* WHUT YOU'RE ASKIN'?

DARREN. Yes!

SHANE. I DON'T *KNOW!*

Fuck!

WHY DOES EV'YBODY KEEP ASKIN' THAT *QUESTION?*

Ever since that stupid *letter* — whut's Shane Mungitt thinkin'? Whut's Shane Mungitt *feelin'?*

How'm I s'pose'ta KNOW?

How'm I s'pose'ta know whut's in my heart?

Fuck, Kippy, why'n't YOU answer for me? Whutever's in there, *you* put it there — not as if I *wrote* that fuckin' letter myself —

DARREN. *(Quickly.)* What? *(Kippy freezes.)*

SHANE. *Shit!* I could hardly *read* that fuckin' letter! There was words in there I did'n' even *know* — *"Onliest"?*

DARREN. You wrote that?

SHANE. Why'd'ya make me *talk?* Why's ev'ybody wanna make me *talk?* An' now ya want me to talk when ya want me to talk an' you want me to *shut up* when ya want me to shut up an' THAT'S NOT *NICE!* —

DARREN. Jesus, Kippy —

SHANE. WHY'N'T YA BOTH JUST LEAVE ME ALONE?

WHY'D YA COME INTO THAT SHOWER?

WHY'D YA WRITE THAT LETTER?

They would'a' let me back — 'venchally — they would'a' just let me back — an' nobody would'a' made me *talk* —
I'M NOT S'POSE'TA TALK! I'M S'POSE'TA *THROW!* AN' NOW THEY WO'N *LET ME* THROW!
FUCKIN' NIGGERS! FUCKIN' QUEERS!
I WANNA *SHUT UP!*
I WANNA THROW! (He starts hammering the table with the fists, unbelievably hard.)
I WANNA THROW! I WANNA THROW! I WANNA THROW!
(A guard enters, grabs and subdues Shane, and leads him out of the room.)
SHANE. *(As he goes.) I! WANNA! THR-O-O-O-O-O-O-W-W-W! (He's gone. Long silence.)*
KIPPY. I-I-I-I-I … *(Pause.)*
I … I … *(Pause.)*
I thought … I knew who he really *was.*
…
…
I thought I was the only one who did. *(Darren looks at him. He walks out of the room. Kippy is alone. Lights.)* Oh, and yeah, we won the World Series.
I know you're supposed to build all sorts of tension around that event but …
We played like maniacs.
Guys didn't talk much; that seemed like the best policy.
We played like Kawabata.
We went at it and went at it and went at it and it didn't mean anything. And that was soothing. *(The guys empty out their lockers, take off. Then Kippy, solo.)*
What happened to Shane was … nothing.
There wasn't really anything to go on; it was all too vague.
He *was* banished from professional baseball, for life this time. Though the way pitching is these days …
He returned home to Arkansas or Tennessee.
And he bought himself a shotgun there.
And one night he and his shotgun went on a tour of the local convenience stores.
And you know how they're putting milk in those glass bottles again? Well Shane Mungitt shot the milk out of every bottle within a ten-mile radius of his house.
He's in jail for *that* now …
Last Looks After the Last Game: *(Lights. The field. Darren is alone*

in the empty ballpark. He's holding a ball, which he rotates absently, gracefully. After a moment, Kippy enters. Silence.) I don't know; this always seems like the wrong weather. *(Beat.)*

DARREN. Huh?

KIPPY. This chilly business, this *nip* in the air. October. It's the wrong weather for baseball, don't you think?

DARREN. It's the right weather for October.

KIPPY. ... Mmm, I guess.

I don't really mean it anyway. I'm just making chat.

Are you going to that party?

DARREN. ... Don't really have a choice.

KIPPY. Well yes, well yes, I guess not

...

What a fuck of a season.

DARREN. ... Nn-hn.

KIPPY. *Fuck* of a season. *(Beat.)*

Will we ever be friends again?

DARREN. Were we ever before?

KIPPY. Yes.

I will doubt everything, but not that.

I refuse.

DARREN. Well.

Maybe we will.

KIPPY. ... Can we at least talk at the party?

DARREN. Ya can't talk at the party, Kippy — it's too loud to talk at the party.

KIPPY. Then can we move our lips at the party and each pretend he understands what the other's saying?

DARREN. Oh, we never had any trouble with *that*, Kippy ... *(Mason enters, delighted.)*

MASON. Is it all right that I'm here?

DARREN. Sure.

MASON. Security *knows* me now — they let me go right on — what about *this*? A few months ago I'd never even seen a game on TV and now I'm *on the field.*

KIPPY. Hi.

MASON. Hi ... oh, *hi!*

DARREN. You two met?

MASON. No — I *recognize* you, of course —

KIPPY. *(Extends hand.)* Christopher Sunderstrom, nice to meet you —

MASON. *(Shaking hands.)* Mars Marzac — *very* nice to meet you — very nice, in*deed. What* a game you had! What a series! What a *rush*, huh? You must be feeling every sort of wonderful right now, yes?

KIPPY. It's a little more complicated than that.

MASON. Oh.

How gauche of me. Of course.

This has been a very difficult year. Of course I realize that. I should stop talking. I'm talking too much. I'm bubbly!

(Barely a hesitation.) The year the Yankees won the Series for the third time, only their fathers kept dying? Someone asked David Cone what the feeling was like in the clubhouse, and he tried to give an answer, but finally he said he really couldn't because it was "kind of tough to eloquate." Isn't that a glorious neologism? Because it's exactly what one tries very hard to do with feelings that are ineffable — first *locate* and then speak *eloquently* about them — and it's an idea that never had a word before so I say: David Cone, I salute you, sir!

It must be like that for *you* now — am I talking too much?

KIPPY. No — no.

We're just ... we're ...

Well, it's kind of tough to eloquate — listen, I'm going to that party. *(To Mason:)* Very good to meet you.

MASON. And you.

KIPPY. *(Turns to Darren.)* I'll see you there later ... my man. *(He exits.)*

MASON. *(Singing.)* "Oh my man, I love him so, he'll never know ... " *(Mason giggles.)*

DARREN. Are you drunk?

MASON. I *had* a beer.

DARREN. You had a keg.

MASON. No. Just one.

The great advantage of an extremely narrow life is the slightest deviation produces *stag*gering results. *(He giggles.)* Oh, I'm sorry if I'm silly.

DARREN. No, it's kinda cute. Kinda endearing ...

MASON. Oh ... well ... yes, it is ...

DARREN. ... So, Mason, I was wonderin' ...

MASON. Yes?

DARREN. If I retire now, will I —

MASON. On no no no no no *no* — not the night you won the World *Series!* My God, man, have you no sense of oc*ca*sion?

DARREN. I just need to be alone for a while.

I just need to get real quiet.

I'm not who I was when the season started.

MASON. Neither am I — isn't it *great?*

DARREN. But, ya see, unlike you, I *liked* who I …

But I guess I really wasn't that then, either.

MASON. … Darren, I truly, deeply feel I should be responding to your *crise* right now but all I keep thinking is when do you get the *ring?*

DARREN. The —

MASON. The championship —

DARREN. Oh, next year.

MASON. Well, then you *have* to come back, you don't have a choice —

DARREN. *(Flashing rings.)* I already have two others.

MASON. Oh! Is *that* what those are?

DARREN. What didja think?

MASON. I didn't know. I just thought you had terrible taste! Wow! Look at them.

DARREN. Yeah —

MASON. Well, all you have to do is look at them and you'll know.

DARREN. Know what?

MASON. Who you are. Your ontological quandary will be dispelled.

DARREN. They just mean I was on a winning team, that's all.

MASON. That's a better start than most of us get. Don't diminish it, it would be too ungrateful.

DARREN. *(Still sad.)* I s'pose. *(Beat.)*

I guess I have to go to this *party*. *(Beat.)*

Do you wanna come?

MASON. Huh?

DARREN. Wanna be my date?

MASON. Don't you have a date?

DARREN. No.

MASON. How can you not have a date?

DARREN. I told you — I don't know people.

MASON. But you didn't mean that.

DARREN. But I did. *(Beat.)*

Come on. We'll get photographed together, splashed over alla tabloids. Everybody'll think you're my long-awaited *boy*friend. Those two gay guys down the hall will drop dead. *(A hitch as he hears this, brief, then:)*

Then I won't haveta kiss you in the elevator like we've both been dreading.

MASON. ... Okay.

Um. Yes!

But do I look ... all right.

DARREN. You look okay.

... You could maybe use an accessory —

MASON. I don't — have —

DARREN. *(Pulling off one of his rings.)* Hey — wear this.

MASON. What?

DARREN. Yeah — it'll be a goof — come on. *(He slips the ring on Mason's finger.)* That feels weird, doesn't it?

MASON. Wow. *(Mason spreads his fingers in front of him to inspect ring.)*

DARREN. Hey, Mars — it's gonna be a roomful of *jocks.* *(He folds his fingers into a fist, demonstrates looking at the ring that way.)*

MASON. Oh ... oh.

DARREN. So — whaddya say?

MASON. Sure. *(He starts to leave with Darren, pauses.)* Um — would it be all right if I met you there? If I stayed here just a little bit longer?

DARREN. You know where the place is?

MASON. I do, in fact.

DARREN. Sure. Enjoy yourself.

MASON. Thank you.

DARREN. Hey — Mars? *(Mason turns to Darren. Darren tosses him the ball. He catches it, gasps.)* What a fuck of a season, huh?

MASON. Yes. It was. A fuck of a season.

It was ... tragic. *(Darren exits. To himself, realizing it.)* It *was* — tragic. *(A moment. His glance falls on the ring. Then moves to the ball. Then he closes his eyes and takes a deep breath, and opens his eyes, and takes in the whole stadium.)* What will we do till spring? *(Fade out.)*

End of Play

PROPERTY LIST

Towels
Clothes (for dressing after showers)
Baseball bat
Sunflower seeds (RODRIGUEZ, MARTINEZ)
Baseball (SKIPPER, DARREN)
Things in lockers (VARIOUS BALLPLAYERS)
Ring (DARREN)

SOUND EFFECTS

Sound of bat hitting ball
Phone ringing
Beep tone

NEW PLAYS

★ **THE EXONERATED by Jessica Blank and Erik Jensen.** Six interwoven stories paint a picture of an American criminal justice system gone horribly wrong and six brave souls who persevered to survive it. "The #1 play of the year...intense and deeply affecting..." *–NY Times.* "Riveting. Simple, honest storytelling that demands reflection." *–A.P.* "Artful and moving...pays tribute to the resilience of human hearts and minds." *–Variety.* "Stark...riveting...cunningly orchestrated." *–The New Yorker.* "Hard-hitting, powerful, and socially relevant." *–Hollywood Reporter.* [7M, 3W] ISBN: 0-8222-1946-8

★ **STRING FEVER by Jacquelyn Reingold.** Lily juggles the big issues: turning forty, artificial insemination and the elusive scientific Theory of Everything in this Off-Broadway comedy hit. "Applies the elusive rules of string theory to the conundrums of one woman's love life. Think *Sex and the City* meets *Copenhagen.*" *–NY Times.* "A funny offbeat and touching look at relationships...an appealing romantic comedy populated by oddball characters." *–NY Daily News.* "Where kooky, zany, and madcap meet...whimsically winsome." *–NY Magazine.* "STRING FEVER will have audience members happily stringing along." *–TheaterMania.com.* "Reingold's language is surprising, inventive, and unique." *–nytheatre.com.* "...[a] whimsical comic voice." *–Time Out.* [3M, 3W (doubling)] ISBN: 0-8222-1952-2

★ **DEBBIE DOES DALLAS adapted by Erica Schmidt, composed by Andrew Sherman, conceived by Susan L. Schwartz.** A modern morality tale told as a comic musical of tragic proportions as the classic film is brought to the stage. "A scream! A saucy, tongue-in-cheek romp." *–The New Yorker.* "Hilarious! DEBBIE manages to have it all: beauty, brains and a great sense of humor!" *–Time Out.* "Shamelessly silly, shrewdly self-aware and proud of being naughty. Great fun!" *–NY Times.* "Racy and raucous, a lighthearted, fast-paced thoroughly engaging and hilarious send-up." *–NY Daily News.* [3M, 5W] ISBN: 0-8222-1955-7

★ **THE MYSTERY PLAYS by Roberto Aguirre-Sacasa.** Two interrelated one acts, loosely based on the tradition of the medieval mystery plays. "... stylish, spine-tingling...Mr. Aguirre-Sacasa uses standard tricks of horror stories, borrowing liberally from masters like Kafka, Lovecraft, Hitchcock...But his mastery of the genre is his own...irresistible." *–NY Times.* "Undaunted by the special-effects limitations of theatre, playwright and *Marvel* comic-book writer Roberto Aguirre-Sacasa maps out some creepy twilight zones in THE MYSTERY PLAYS, an engaging, related pair of one acts...The theatre may rarely deliver shocks equivalent to, say, *Dawn of the Dead*, but Aguirre-Sacasa's work is fine compensation." *–Time Out.* [4M, 2W] ISBN: 0-8222-2038-5

★ **THE JOURNALS OF MIHAIL SEBASTIAN by David Auburn.** This epic one-man play spans eight tumultuous years and opens a uniquely personal window on the Romanian Holocaust and the Second World War. "Powerful." *–NY Times.* "[THE JOURNALS OF MIHAIL SEBASTIAN] allows us to glimpse the idiosyncratic effects of that awful history on one intelligent, pragmatic, recognizably real man..." *–NY Newsday.* [3M, 5W] ISBN: 0-8222-2006-7

★ **LIVING OUT by Lisa Loomer.** The story of the complicated relationship between a Salvadoran nanny and the Anglo lawyer she works for. "A stellar new play. Searingly funny." *–The New Yorker.* "Both generous and merciless, equally enjoyable and disturbing." *–NY Newsday.* "A bitingly funny new comedy. The plight of working mothers is explored from two pointedly contrasting perspectives in this sympathetic, sensitive new play." *–Variety.* [2M, 6W] ISBN: 0-8222-1994-8

DRAMATISTS PLAY SERVICE, INC.
440 Park Avenue South, New York, NY 10016 212-683-8960 Fax 212-213-1539
postmaster@dramatists.com www.dramatists.com